Psychology Revivals

Coupling…
What Makes Permanence?

Originally published in 1991, the theme for this title is the exploration of the components of lasting, long-term relationships. It begins with the first part of an interview between Sheldon Starr and Virginia Satir, made in 1985 and is followed by a comment on that interview by the Editor. Other chapters discuss the subject of falling in love and the notion of 'being in love' as distinguished from 'a love relationship'. The authors, including some who have been married for many years themselves, look at the many aspects that make long-term relationships successful. The chapters range in essence from 'What is love?' to 'How is love maintained?'. This title aims to share the information the authors have gained, about what makes coupling work, with society as a whole.

Coupling…
What Makes Permanence?

Edited by
Barbara Jo Brothers

Routledge
Taylor & Francis Group
LONDON AND NEW YORK

First published in 1991
by The Haworth Press, Inc.

This edition first published in 2015 by Routledge
27 Church Road, Hove BN3 2FA

and by Routledge
711 Third Avenue, New York, NY 10017

Routledge is an imprint of the Taylor & Francis Group, an informa business

Publisher's Note
The publisher has gone to great lengths to ensure the quality of this reprint but points out that some imperfections in the original copies may be apparent.

Disclaimer
The publisher has made every effort to trace copyright holders and welcomes correspondence from those they have been unable to contact.

A Library of Congress record exists under ISBN: 1560241861

ISBN: 978-1-138-81418-9 (hbk)
ISBN: 978-1-315-74705-7 (ebk)

Coupling . . . What Makes Permanence?

Barbara Jo Brothers
Editor

The Haworth Press
New York • London • Sydney

Coupling . . . What Makes Permanence? has also been published as *Journal of Couples Therapy*, Volume 2, Number 3 1991.

The Haworth Press, Inc. 10 Alice Street, Binghamton, NY 13904-1580
Haworth/EUROSPAN, 3 Henrietta Street, London WC2E 8LU England
Haworth/ASTAM, 162-168 Parramatta Road, Stanmore, Sydney, N.S.W. 2048 Australia

Library of Congress Cataloging-in-Publication Data

Coupling – what makes permanence? / Barbara Jo Brothers, editor.
p. cm.
"Coupling – what makes permanence? has also been published as Journal of couples therapy, volume 2, number 3, 1991" – T.p. verso.
ISBN 1-56024-186-1 (alk. paper)
1. Marriage. 2. Interpersonal relations. I. Brothers, Barbara, 1940– .
HQ734.C8656 1991
306.81 – dc20 91-23880
CIP

Coupling . . .
What Makes Permanence?

CONTENTS

∞ ALL HAWORTH BOOKS & JOURNALS ARE PRINTED ON CERTIFIED ACID-FREE PAPER

ABOUT THE EDITOR

Barbara Jo Brothers, MSW, BCD, a Diplomate in Clinical Social Work, National Association of Social Workers, is in private practice in New Orleans. She received her BA from the University of Texas and her MSW from Tulane University, where she is currently on the faculty. She was editor *The Newsletter of the American Academy of Psychotherapists* from 1976 to 1985, and was associate editor of *Voices: The Art and Science of Psychotherapy* from 1979 to 1989. She has nearly 30 years of experience, in both the public and private sectors, helping people to form skills that will enable them to connect emotionally. The author of numerous articles and book chapters on authenticity in human relating, she has advocated healthy, congruent communication that builds intimacy as opposed to destructive, incongruent communication which blocks intimacy. In addition to her many years of direct work with couples and families, Ms. Brothers has led numerous workshops on teaching communication in families and has also played an integral role in the development of training programs in family therapy for mental health workers throughout the Louisiana state mental health system. She is a board member of the Institute of International Connections, a non-profit organization for cross-cultural professional development, focused on training for Soviet psychotherapists and cross-cultural Soviet-American exchange.

Coupling . . .
What Makes Permanence?

Introduction

Barbara Jo Brothers

> . . . for love in action is a harsh and dreadful thing compared to love in dream.
>
> –Dostoyevsky, 1950, p. 65

The theme for this volume is the exploration of the components of lasting, long term relationships; authentic, generative connection as opposed to a sort of coalition of misery–the uneasy, frantic shifting for balance currently being described as "co-dependency."

The volume begins with the first segment of an interview between Sheldon Starr and Virginia Satir, made in 1985. This the first installment of a several part series to be continued throughout the next several volumes; the whole piece is long and rich in content.

Although the subject of the interview was, ostensibly, the training of family therapists, Virginia, in her characteristic way, spoke to the larger picture: the training of the human being for *being* human. If therapists are to be change agents on behalf of those they see in therapy, their own eyes need to be cleared of the mists from the inhuman rules which almost all of us learn from our early childhood experiences. As the United States and allied troops began the bombing of Iraq while this volume was coalescing, the urgency of the heightened violence in the world became even greater impetus to emphasize the importance of exchanging the inhuman rules for human ones; for understanding what *does* work in the facilitation of human bonding and to make that knowledge available to greater populations. This urgency lies behind my own editorial, "Ask Not for Whom the Siren Wails." As therapists, the readers of this volume do have access to the information about what makes coupling work, what makes families thrive, what makes it possible for group members to resolve differences without killing each other. We need to find expedient ways to get that information out to the rest of society; this need becomes more urgent with every war that passes.

In the context of several short articles, Howard Halpern and six other therapists share thoughts on the subject of falling in love, struggling to separate the dross from the gold in that phenomenon. Howard Halpern addresses the popular notion of "being in love," distinguishing between "a love relationship" and love as a subjective feeling. Several members of the editorial board give their various reflections on Halpern's thoughts. Griffin deepens the discussion further by picking out the theme of *longing* and its potential constructive application in the opening of closed selves or souls in preparation for the possible participation in a love relationship. Ansell is concerned about the danger of making to sound trivial the seriousness of narcissism versus mature, generative love. Lathrop speaks to the point of "being in love" as projection of one's own idealized and unrealized potentials. Travers would rather define love as a decision—"an act of the will translated into action . . . a life orientation, to be a loving person." Sam and Diane Kirschner bring "being in love" down to earth in pointing to the cycling of inner child and adult sides of the two members of the couple. In essence, seven therapists have put their heads together to speak to the definition of love—something that has not occurred with great frequency in professional literature.

Highly qualified to address the issue of long-term relating because of their own forty-plus years of marriage and working together, the Schwartzes profile three different couples' styles of staying together; they write of the importance of giving up illusion and dealing with the fear of loss as integral parts of the process. Perry builds on the theme by adding the importance of the "web of trust" which is woven in the therapeutic process to mitigate the fear of loss; dialogue in the safety of the therapist's office is not necessarily prey to the unskilled communication styles which may feed fear and alienation in the couple proceeding in dialogue on their own.

Al Jasnow is another therapist with several decades of satisfying marriage behind him. Jasnow, with his long term perspective, looks at the difference culture makes on marital and coupling styles. Viewing the modern couple relationship as "tremendously complex," he sees flexibility as the key—the ability to coordinate mutual needs for dependence and independence which is based on self awareness, self acceptance and self esteem. The choice of permanence in relationship has a different meaning in these modern times in which certain kinds of choice have been greatly extended from the days in which people rarely ventured more than thirty miles from their homes. In earlier times, one lived much more closely with *whatever* decisions one made, living with the same 200 to 300 family groups day in and day out as was the case in the agrarian society of a few generations ago.

The Perls are a long term married and long term partnered-as-therapists couple. They describe the experience of their own group of personal friends, all married at least thirty years; a thoughtful examination polling, on an informal basis, the experience of long term married couples. It is the enlightened musing of an experienced therapist: what accounts for the longevity of the relationships and the apparent long term success of the marriages? Common interests mingled well with separate, individual interests pursued by each member of the pair seem to emerge as important in the collection of shared factors.

Golden discusses the relationship of the instinctual drive of attachment from the point of view of that which is functional as opposed to that which is dysfunctional. Bringing a refreshing respect for the patient/client/person, she also brings a deeper (and more humane) level of understanding of the attraction the abused often retains to the abuser in the face of extreme unhappy and dangerous conditions. Understanding of attachment in terms of basic drive for survival puts a whole new light on that which has been otherwise rather derisively labeled "co-dependent" behavior.

Clarkson's very rich study of the components of permanence in the coupling process provides a thoughtful examination of the five facets universal to all healthy long-term couple relationships, defining the person-to-person aspect, the transferential aspect, the working alliance, the reparative aspect, and including the transpersonal aspect. Her belief is, while good relationships may exist in which all five facets are not necessarily encompassed, they must all five be present "for the jewel of human love to reach its full brilliance."

Clarkson's article, like Golden's is characterized by her merciful and respectful attitude toward struggling humanity.

Jerry Travers takes a whimsical tact in distinguishing between the patterns that move a couple toward divorce, versus those that are essential in moving a couple toward a healthy style of relating. He outlines a guaranteed route toward divorce as well as considering the ingredients in longevity of relationship.

Scher shares his subjective observations, based on his experience as a twenty-six year "veteran" of marriage, about the ingredients in the maintenance of a marriage in the face of the illusions with which most people enter that contract. Pearlmutter adds her opinion, diverging on the subject of autonomy in relationships, concerned that the degree of autonomy Scher advocates requires more differentiation of self than most couples reach.

Thus the articles may be said to range, in essence, from "What is love?" to "How is love maintained?" There is a consensus flowing through all the articles that balancing adult needs and child needs is one key; recognizing the pervasive illusory factors is another. Perhaps the need for attachment which Golden has brought to our attention plays a much more important role than we have realized—the legitimate longing any human being experiences to feel safe and protected from the very real vicissitudes the world does hold. That *instinctual* need provides a convincing explanation for the otherwise puzzling coalitions of misery.

Which brings us back to the inter-relatedness of all things: safe babies grow up to be relying and reliable spouses. Would that our world might sooner than later see the value of placing the safety of *all* babies above *all* other priorities.

REFERENCE

Dostoyevsky, F. (1950). *The Brothers Karamazov*. New York: Random House.

An Interview with Virginia Satir

Sheldon Starr

[Early in 1985 I asked Virginia Satir if she was willing to be interviewed on videotape concerning her thinking about family therapy at that time and especially with regard to any ideas she might wish to share with the family therapy community. The interview took place on March 15, 1985 at Virginia's home in Menlo Park, California. The transcript of the interview is 60 pages, and this is the first of a series of segments from that interview covering different themes. This segment concerns the person of the therapist in family therapy training.]

STARR: You are the only renowned family therapist I know of who goes right to the consumer. You fill up auditoriums with non-therapist types. What for?

SATIR: A long time ago I saw no reason why the information that we as therapists had should be kept precious. *I think that what we know everybody else needs to know, in the same way that mathematicians don't have to keep the multiplication tables to themselves.*

Sheldon Starr, PhD, was founder and director for 15 years of the Family Study Unit, a family therapy training and treatment program at the V.A. Medical Center, Palo Alto, CA when this interview was conducted. Dr. Starr is presently Professor of Psychology (part time) at Pacific Graduate School of Psychology and is in private practice, both in Palo Alto, CA. His association with Virginia Satir spanned 25 years, first as student, then as associate and long-time friend. Correspondence may be sent to 801 Welch Road, #209, Palo Alto, CA 94304.

This paper is a highly condensed and edited summary of the entire interview which appeared in the AFTA Newsletter, Fall 1985 and that version consisted of less than 20% of the interview.

[The use of brackets [] and italics are editorial additions for the purpose of clarity and emphasis.]

That's number one. [Second], I have always wanted to help people to develop a better state of their own consciousness and a better appreciation of themselves. I like people, and I believe in them. *I have never thought of people as objects, so I know that people can grow.* Often what people say to me is, "There's something about your presence that makes me feel okay about me," and when I hear that, I feel so glad, because what I worry about is that people will feel good *because* of me or that they will feel good because they think I made them feel good *rather* than that they begin to feel good themselves because of what we've developed. This may sound real shocking to some people, but for me, *being a professional is being the best human being that I can be, and joining all human beings where they are*. You're coming to me not because I'm better than you are, but because I can see your blind spots, and you can't see them. I might have something to offer that you haven't yet learned about yourself. I can help you to get in touch with some things, but this has nothing to do with how we look at and value each other. So there is that kind of feeling. And I go into this kind of detail, because that *therapeutic cloak* which many of us in the therapy field have worn, has said in early years, "Don't put yourself in it, just walk in [wearing] your cloak and be an objective clinician." I can't do that.

STARR: You're charismatic and you have impact on people. Suppose young aspiring therapists feel that they want to do that like you, but they're not you?

SATIR: First of all, let me tell you something about training. Today the main training that goes on, has very little to do with helping the therapist in-training to *become more fully human.* It doesn't happen! What trainers forget is that it's *not* our techniques, it's our person, and then the use of our techniques in relation to people. So I meet a lot of young beautiful people and it's not a question of being like *me*, it's a question of what you look at. I'll give you a little anecdote. You know I was one of the people, perhaps the first one in California to go to the back wards of the State Hospitals and ask for [patients] who had families, and I interviewed them. Within ten weeks most of them left the hospital. Okay?

STARR: That's fantastic!

SATIR: That happened, it helped develop things [my thinking about individuals in relation to their family system]. Alright, now people [the professionals] would say to me, "You know, maybe we made a mistake in diagnosis." I said, 'No you didn't. You didn't make a mistake in diagnosis.' "Well what lead you to that [how you intervened]?" What I look at [not diagnosis] leads me to something else. I look at you as a being who is struggling to free yourself, and the particular ways you're doing it aren't getting you there, and we have [invent] a name for it. We call it schizophrenia, or we call it manic-depressive or we can call it whatever we want. Alright? Now, *if I get stuck on that label instead of seeing how can I help you to free your energy,* [*nothing will happen*]. [The question is] how can I touch you, how can I have you touch me, how can I look at you, how can you look at me, how can we use the things that human beings have in the world, which are in their hearts, their heads, their bodies, their sights, their sounds, and their hearing? How can we do that inner touching so that you begin to free [yourself]? How can I then, work with family systems in relation to this and family members to help this happen? *And the point of all of it has to do with the fact that the real thing that I need to pay attention to is our humanness and the only thing that is going to change anything is going to be you tapping into your own resources.*

STARR: How do you train people to be human? Is that even possible?

SATIR: Oh yes it is! Absolutely possible! You want my fantasy about it and my reality about it?

STARR: Yes indeed.

SATIR: The first thing I would do is help the therapists get in touch with all the messages they learned when they were growing up about how they should be. Then, I would lead them all through Family Reconstructions so that they could become free of those messages. And I would talk to them about anything about [their own] families. They would all work on that so they would have a chance to take a look at what was going on. We would avoid things like I have seen with some trainers and trainees [in a family training institute]. A husband, wife, and child were treated by a trainee and there was the kind of thing that went on between husband and wife where the husband was looking like he had to "cow-tow" to the wife so to speak, and this male therapist finally cut off, even sat in front of the woman, and was taking the husband's side. Okay. So when he [the therapist] came out [of the interview room] I said, 'How was that experience for you?' He said, "Terrible. I can't . . . those people aren't treatable, *especially* the woman." So then I waited a little bit and said, 'Where'd you meet them before?' Well as it turned out, this had been "his family," and that's what [his taking sides] exactly was [about]. *All of us at this point in time in the history of the world, with very few exceptions, were brought up in such a way that we all have messages that are against our growth.* Like, "don't be angry with someone that you love"; "don't show anybody that you don't know every thing"; "don't ask for what you want or somebody will be upset." Or, "don't be."

STARR: I see that one depress people when they get the message, "don't be."

SATIR: Sure. So you see what I do with therapists is acquaint them, first of all, with their own [family] messages and help them to go beyond them, *because a therapist who is working, who doesn't know that he has these, can do frightful things to patients. So I work on the person of the therapist and help them to get in touch with where they are and what their family rules are about.*

STARR: What you're saying isn't just fantasy. In the family training program I direct everyone has to do a family life chronology and we typically do family reconstructions. When we rehash our sessions what we go over is the person of the therapist. "Now who does the father in that family remind you of?"

SATIR: Well, see that's what I started in training.

STARR: It's not completely fantasy.

SATIR: Well it's fantasy to the degree that when you want to prepare a therapist, that this is where you start. That's not yet natural [typical of training]. And I know persons like yourself and others are doing it.

STARR: Okay but that's the exception, not the rule.

SATIR: You're the exception, not the rule . . . that's a better way of saying it, that is the exception not the rule . . .

Ask Not for Whom the Siren Wails

Barbara Jo Brothers

SUMMARY. Comment on an interview conducted with Virginia Satir by Sheldon Starr (1985). Included is a discussion on the relationship between the training of psychotherapists and avoiding wars. Not thinking of people as objects has enormous implications; mutual respect is the operative ingredient.

> . . . the real thing that I [we] need to pay attention to is our humanness . . .
>
> – Virginia Satir, 1985

As I put together the final pages of this volume dedicated to the exploration and fostering of human bonding and enhancing of intimacy between the dyad, the world stands witness to the antithesis of human bonding, the ultimate in human estrangement: war. Mega-level war. The point of this particular volume is the exploration of what makes the human union last – and last on a constructive and enriching track as opposed to being locked into the slow death of a pact born of a balance of mutual misery.

While we all hope this war will be history by the time this volume sees the light of day, nevertheless, is chilling evidence that there may be no moment more important in human history in which to ask the question: what transforms a human union into a loving union that emotionally *sustains* the pair? What makes an interaction a growth-enhancing one? What are the ingredients of conflict resolution from which both people walk away alive and whole. Such resolution *is* a possibility in human affairs, although clearly the more challenging route.

There is, of course, survival value in loyalty to one's group and willingness to fight off predators. Elephant cows circle their young and elephant bulls circle the smaller circle, thus repelling less intelligent predators by mammalian group effort. Baboons do a variation of the same thing. When human beings first crept out on Africa's savannahs, the loyalty to fellow humanoid comrades did serve to protect the small, vulnerable bands from the saber-toothed tigers. What is required now is to make the tribal mentality leap from the artificial construct "nation" to the entire human race as tribe.

At this point in history, we are literally linked electronically. During World War II, the telephone reception was so bad that my grandmother and mother had to make their telephone calls at a prearranged time in order to even know for sure it was the related person on the other end of the line. We lived not more than 15 miles apart. Less than 12 hours after the initial bombing of Iraq, my cousin in Riyadh, called his mother in Texas to reassure her about his well-being. He calls, now, after each alarming report of bombing from where he is in Saudi Arabia. I have a friend in Moscow and a friend in Lithuania and telephone numbers for both. We all see the small Israeli child begin to cry as his mother insistently and anxiously buckles on his gas mask. A beautiful little Jordanian girl shows up in my living room, courtesy of CNN. Age 9, she says yes, she would be quite glad to have, as friend, the little Israeli boy who appears in the same interview; no, no, she says, she does not like this war. This is not the same world as 1941; jet planes and microchips make physical borders meaningless.

Virginia Satir's deceptively simple message as expressed in the interview elsewhere in this volume: the world needs the information about human dynamics that the mental health professions have distilled is increased in poignance, the U.S.A. having just begun to lead a multi-nation allied war against the leader of Iraq.

> . . . What we know, everybody else needs to know. It's the same way that mathematicians don't have to keep the multiplication tables to themselves . . .

If that was true January 15, 1991, it was true in spades the night of January 16, 1991. We have certainly passed around among us all such information in higher mathematics, physics, chemistry, and engineering to make it technologically possible to create destruction at a several hundred mile range; any human being whose personality structure is organized in such a manner as to permit him or her to garner the necessary political power is able to do so.

> First, one of the things I have long since wanted [is] to help people develop a better state of their *own consciousness*, a better appreciation of themselves, and a feel of the psychology [the mental/bio-chemical/spiritual processes from] which [the disciplines of] psychiatry, social work, and psychology—and the whole of all learning—comes from. (1985)

Perhaps, if the world—news media, governments and populations, *as well as* psychotherapists—could be as interested and informed in the understanding of the way the human being operates as it has been in the way Scud missiles and anti-Scud, Patriot missiles operate, the firing back and forth of both could recede in importance.

> Second . . . I like people and I believe in them and I *have never thought of people as objects* . . .

Here is an example of the deceptive simplicity of Virginia's profound insight into human behavior. Not thinking of people as objects has enormous implications. It is much more difficult to shoot an entity one perceives to be another human being than it is to fire at "a target." There was much talk of this during the time U.S. hostages were being held in Iran in the 1980's: that ripple of fear seeing them blindfolded—the eyes, which all of us are aware carry the essence of human facial feature, covered over. Human intercourse is deeply affected by whether one or both are treating each other as objects rather than fellow creatures with hearts and soul.

This choice of relating to whole person rather than object is directly related to feelings of self-worth:

> . . . the more you appreciate yourself, the less you will have to depreciate anyone else. Put another way, the more you can appreciate yourself, the more you can appreciate others. (Satir, 1986, tape 1)

Virginia Satir believed that a focus on the human-ness in the human being was an essential factor in being a professional.

> . . . this may sound real shocking to some people, but, for me, really being a professional is first of all being the best human being that I can be and to join all human beings where they are . . .

Joining all human beings, sharing our common humanity—expanding our essential tribal mentality to include the entire race as one tribe—cuts through artificial divisions of nationality, social class, and the more subtle, finely tuned, but equally "class-ist" hierarchal attitudes: distinctions of client or patient versus therapist. "Joining all human beings where they are" has powerful possibilities for creating environment for mutual understanding.

It was Virginia's well-considered opinion that training for the role of therapist should not be separated from the role of responsible human being. In her mind, the kind of information needed in training for professional treatment of human interaction was not substantially different from the kind of information required for growth-enhancing interaction among any group of human beings. This was, of course, particularly radical in those white-coated days when psychoanalysis was king of the mental health realm, but is no less true today. Joining is much more important than dividing. *Who* we are carries all the impact in regard to *what* we do.

> . . . even today, the main . . . training that goes on has very little to do with helping the person who is the instrument of passing on this training, namely the therapist to *become more fully human*. It doesn't happen. What people forget: *it's not our techniques, it's our person* and then the use of our techniques in relation to people [that makes the difference] . . . the only thing that is going to change anything is going to be you tapping into your own resources . . .

Virginia's "course of study" in her process communities which constituted her major intensive training formats, were structured to facilitate personal growth of the therapist-participant along those becoming-more-fully-human lines.

> . . . The first thing I would do is to help them get in touch with all the messages they learned when they were growing up about how they should be . . . then I would lead them all through family reconstructions so that they could be free of those messages . . . with very few exceptions [we] were brought up in such a way that we all have messages that are against our growth. Like: Don't be angry against somebody that you love; don't show anybody that you don't know everything; don't ask for what you want or somebody will be upset . . .

This idea Virginia held that therapists must work on their own issues is, of course, hardly new. The aforementioned psychoanalysts have held that position for generations now and there is agreement, even among the disciplines in which it is not a requirement, that such inner exploration of one's own inner territory is essential to the performance of good therapy.

She goes on to say:

> What I have to do with therapists is acquaint them, first of all, with their own messages that they got, help them to go beyond them, because a therapist who is working who doesn't know that he has these can do frightful things to patients. So I work on the *person of the therapist* . . .

Therapy for therapists may not be a unique idea. Focus on the essence of *becoming* a *human being* (as opposed to methods for manipulation by well-honed techniques), is, however, certainly not necessarily the prevailing norm in the therapy world – and less so in the greater human community. Virginia abhorred the treatment of people as objects. She considers this objectifying of another human to be seriously contra-human/counter-therapeutic. Refusing to even use the word "techniques" to describe any of her therapeutic processes, she would choose the word "vehicle" instead. What lay behind her adamancy: in Virginia's view, holding the view of human beings as objects – however ostensibly good the reason – held the danger of "the ends justifying the means" mentality which can easily slide to "To save the village, we had to destroy it." If the therapist can do "frightful things" out of a focus on learning a set of techniques rather than learning the intricacies of her or his early messages, neglecting to relate to the richness of unique personhood, imagine what the rest of the world can do? Unfortunately, we do not have to imagine. We are all watching it via satellite television.

In my own view, the luxury of our being able to continue to treat each other as if we were *not* each one absolutely unique and rich stores of realized and not yet realized potential may be fast running out. Technology may be chasing us toward the choice point: *one* world where we agree to engage in mutual negotiation rather than heavy-handed power plays . . . or *no* world: blown apart by some grim miscalculation between the arsenals of terrorists and would-be liberators. The "smart" bombs do not care one shrapnel piece on whom they fall.

Mutual respect could, quite literally, be our next-to-the-last-choice.

REFERENCES

Satir, V. *Speaker*. (1985). An Interview with Virginia Satir by Sheldon Starr, PhD. (Available from Sheldon Starr, PhD, 801 Welch Road, #209, Palo Alto, CA 94304.)

Satir, V. *Speaker*. (1986). (Avanta Process Community 6, Module I). Crested Butte, Co: Blue Moon Cassettes. Cassette Recording #1.

Feeling in Love Is Not Enough

Howard Halpern

I used to argue with people who used the word love when discussing destructive, frustrating or futile relationships. Love is not supposed to be a miserable feeling. Then I thought, "Who am I to argue with someone who says he is in love? How can I deny what he experiences?" If people say they feel love, they feel love. I may want to point out other related factors such as obsession or possessiveness or addiction or infatuation, but I can't say, "What you feel is not love."

I do, however, make a clear distinction between a love relationship and love as a subjective feeling. A romantic love relationship requires many things that the love feeling alone does not. The feeling of being in love requires only one person, a love relationship requires two. A love relationship requires high degrees of mutual caring, sharing, respect and involvement. It requires a degree of availability, of mutual passion, and a desire to be together. It requires that both be committed to struggle to make their coupleness as good as it can get. Love relationships should make people feel better about themselves, not worse. It should make both parties confident they can count on and trust the other.

In other words, the feeling of being in love is not enough to support a love relationship. I believe John Hinckley when he said he loves Jody Foster, a woman he never met, but it is a meaningless emotion when compared with a love relationship requiring mutual knowledge and caring. I believe Jeanne Harris when she says she loved Herman Tarnower, the Scarsdale diet doctor she murdered,

Howard Halpern, PhD, is affiliated with the Apthorp, 2211 Broadway, New York, NY 10024.

but a love relationship implies commitment to the other's well-being, not destructive behavior.

I believe a woman who says she loves a husband who has shown her no kindness by word or action for a decade, but there is no love relationship without kindness, protectiveness and mutual respect.

Unfortunately, some people who are incapable of enjoying and committing themselves to a love relationship are very able to make others fall in love with them. Perhaps they are too self-involved, too afraid of closeness or too consumed by anger and hatred to sustain a love relationship. Trying to have a mutual love relationship with such a person is like asking the Venus de Milo to hug you, but many are locked into the task of trying, and the intensity of this effort can make them feel passionately in love.

So when someone tells me he is enduring an awful, unfulfilling relationship because he is "in love," I say, "I believe you, but so what?" The feeling of love does not in itself indicate that a love relationship exists or that fulfilling coupling is happening.

It is a useful distinction. Being in a love relationship without the feeling of being in love can be deadening. Feeling in love without there being a love relationship can be deadly. Being in love within a love relationship is a blessing.

Comment – Response to Howard Halpern's Article: "Feeling in Love Is Not Enough"

Carol L. Griffin

Feeling in love may not be sufficient for developing and maintaining an intimate love relationship, but it can, nevertheless, have significant value. The feeling described in Dr. Halpern's article is longing, which can arouse a major opening in a hitherto closed soul or self – a spiritual awakening that may precede the ability to participate in a love relationship.

By my observation, most couples fall short of being in love within a love relationship. Many are in relationships devoid of love, often for the purpose of avoiding aloneness and denying loneliness. The result is that each partner then experiences the confusion of loneliness when not actually alone. Of course, loneliness does not require that a person be alone, but if one is alone, it is possible to understand the feeling and to initiate change.

The experience of longing, although it may be unrealistic, allows the self to acknowledge its loneliness. The period of longing required to achieve openness to love, varies for each person, depending upon his/her prior experience of love. But to devalue this feeling is to do a disservice to the self and its needs. If a person is willing to explore the longing, he/she can begin to understand the depths of the soul.

This longing may be necessary before a closed self can truly enter into a mutual loving relationship. The longing allows the self to have a concept of unconditional loving of someone other than oneself. And the pain that is experienced is an indication of one's sense

Carol L. Griffin, in private practice in New York City, has recently legally changed her name to Carol Mary Alexana.

of worthiness to be loved. If the person has not previously felt capable of being loved, his/her progress through this longing can lead to the idea that being loved is possible. An aware therapist can support this movement so that the individual can grow into a loving person capable of being in a true love relationship.

Longing can have another purpose as well. In the progression from personal love to universal love, it can allow the individual to expand his/her concept of love, such that love and understanding of all things does not depend upon personally feeling loved in return (i.e., I love for the sake of loving, not because I expect love or anything else in return). In this case, on a personal love level, one can love someone with whom there is not a "love relationship," but there is enough caring to respect the other's needs even if that need is not to be in a mutual relationship. When this concept expands to a universal love level, an individual can truly experience Eric Fromm's Art of Loving because the love of all others fills the soul with joy.

From my personal experience and observation, the path of truly loving goes from the personal love level to a universal love level which allows an openness to then have a more fulfilling experience of personal love in a healthy, mutual relationship. Therefore, the longing can provide direction for each individual to discover his or her own path of love and possibility of relationship.

REFERENCE

Fromm, E. (1956). *The Art of Loving*. New York: Harper & Row.

Comment – Response To Howard Halpern's Article: "Feeling in Love Is Not Enough"

Charles Ansell

Halpern has listed a number of truisms. They seem inarguable. But it is also a thoughtful statement, except as the work of a trained therapist, truisms are not enough.

As professionals we speak in our own distinctive universe of discourse. We speak a special language to identify problems that we come upon in the human condition.

I would understand Halpern at a deeper level if—for example—he were to speak in the special terms by which we zero in on a problem in human behavior. Thus, for example, if Halpern spoke about the narcissism of childhood that often perseverates into adulthood, I would then understand him to say that the language of the narcissist often misleads us. The narcissistic personality might complain about his need for love but he would be without an awareness of his own inability to accept the other's narcissistic needs.

Informal writing or speaking about love between persons may often achieve eloquence, but it inspires more than it teaches. I suspect that there is a curious reaction among certain professionals that leads them to turn away from a universe of discourse because it might separate them from common understanding. It is as if to speak in truisms is to achieve a kind of philosophic tone that raises our level of understanding onto higher peaks.

Charles Ansell, PhD, 3815 Woodcliff Rd., Sherman Oaks, CA 91403 is in private practice.

It is sad enough that glib media psychologists spout the wildest generalizations over the air waves, intending to impress their listeners with capsules of wisdom. And they are often intriguing. But alas their capsuled wisdoms too often is like the legendary Chinese dinner that leaves you hungry an hour later.

Comment – Response To Howard Halpern's Article: "Feeling in Love Is Not Enough"

Donald Lathrop

Howard Halpern's brief, intense piece says wonderfully what I think, feel, say, and live. I use different words (romantic love for "being in love"; and the love that comes from living it together, that includes mutual respect, that involves both people giving of themselves to their maximum capacity for "love relationship"). I want to add some observations.

Being in love, romantic love, is a delusional state in a normal, healthy human being. It is based 90 + % on projection of one's own inner idealized version of one's undeveloped, unlived contrasexual side. The other 10%, which is rarely that much, is based upon perception of the other, including the other's undeveloped potential. Being in love is a possessed state. That is, normal ego consciousness is nowhere around. It is an intoxication which, like drugs, anesthetizes the higher, most recently developed parts of the personality. People get addicted to this intoxicant. Our society, via Hollywood and Madison Avenue, endorses this addiction as part of our Peter Pan ethic. Most people get married in this possessed state. They then must suffer horrible feelings of betrayal when the "honeymoon is over." If there is enough glue of any kind to hold them

Don Lathrop, MD, is a medical psychotherapist (psychiatrist) in private practice in Boise, ID. He was involved in several capacities with the editorial board of *Voices: The Act and Science of Psychotherapy* for twenty-seven years and is co-editor of *The Relationship Newsletter*. Correspondence may be sent to: 111 W. Curling, Boise, ID 83702.

together, and if both are willing to "grow up," the possibility of developing a love relationship exists.

The purpose of marriage, of a committed, ultimately monogamous, intimate love relationship is to force and foster the development of the undeveloped, originally projected aspects of both personalities.

A Grammar of Love

Jerome A. Travers

There was once a school of thought in epistemology, a branch of philosophy, during the late Middle Ages called Nominalism. The Nominalists believed that concepts were devoid of content, that universal ideas did not exist and that only by attaching a name to a thing does its reality come into being. To these skeptics all naming is relative and individualistic; so that the fruit that you will call an apple I might call an orange, and each of us is equally correct and each name is true.

A type of Nominalism occurs in *Alice in Wonderland* when the Mad Hatter begins to attach arbitrary names to objects with the self confidence which says, "I can call a thing by any name whatsoever and that makes it true!"

What a person calls love does not make it love just because they say so. It is a perversion of language to agree with a client in therapy that their adolescent infatuations, narcissistic questings, infantile craving or masturbatory indulgences are love. Is it not intellectually dishonest to say, for the sake of total client acceptance, "Who am I to say . . . ?" Things do not exist in themselves. Snow is not sand and trees are not cars. To call love a feeling is a perversion of language, an umbrella term which signifies and clarifies nothing.

Love is not a feeling but a verb, and an active verb at that. Romantic fluttering is a feeling; so is being needy, and craving the affection we hope is offered is a feeling. Being sexually stimulated

Jerome A. Travers, PhD, is a psychologist and marriage therapist in Summit, NJ and New York City. Correspondence may be addressed to 7 Ridge Rd., Summit, NJ 07901.

and wanting our depression lifted is a feeling; swooning dizzily in what Freud called a 'transient psychosis' is a feeling. Love is not a feeling, romance is.

Love is a verb, not a noun. Talking about love is cheap, doing it is a challenge. What does it mean that folks no longer write love letters but send buck and a quarter Valentines instead? Substance gets lost in packaging. The Bible says about people who love: "By their deeds ye shall know them." So let's not talk about love, show me!

Does saying "I love you" have much to do with love? Probably not. What it simply means is that "I feel good about myself when I am in your presence." This is a statement about me, not you, not a recognition of the other. Mother Teresa might be one cranky tyrant that you'd prefer not to have a candle light dinner with. But she is the one picking up dying infants on the alleys of Calcutta. That's love. A parent who sits up a night with a sick child, rising above one's own exhaustion to soothe the child, that's love. Acting to foster the growth, freedom and autonomy of one's mate, that's love. Being horny, a doormat, passive, delusional, needy, dependent, emotionally hungry, that's not love.

Love is a decision, an act of the will, translated into action. This decision is a life orientation, to be a loving person. It is rooted in one's own experience of being relatively nurtured and capable of nurturing myself. Charity, love, begins at home, within myself. Loving comes from my abundance of self good feelings, from my overflow. When I'm in a nurtured state I am not manipulative; my narcissism does not become wrapped in altruism.

In esteeming myself, I develop the ability to move outside myself, to supraindividuate, to move from a state of autonomy towards extending oneself into service in a world of causes, institutions and concerns greater than myself. This move from self to supraself provides a balance away from self absorption. It helps me to move civilization one step forward.

Love requires balancing these two creative impulses; the quest to be whole and the need to rise above self for the good of others. Love accepts soberly the limitations of the beloved. "By their deeds you shall know them." Visiting the sick, helping the hurting, feeding the poor, welcoming the stranger, being an instrument of peace; this is love in action.

Love is that total fundamental human act which integrates everything else, helping us to become more human. So no Valentines, thanks; but a short note is welcomed.

The Dual Paths of Healthy Relationships

Diana Adile Kirschner
Sam Kirschner

Howard Halpern has offered an interesting distinction between a "love relationship" and "feeling in love." However, he seems to contradict himself somewhat in the article. He initially states that a love relationship is characterized by high degrees of mutual caring, respect and passion. Later in the closing paragraph, he states that "being in a love relationship without the feeling of being in love can be deadening." Despite the confusing terminology, Halpern's point is an important one since people often confuse the feelings of being in love with the behaviors, cognitions, and feelings of being in a fulfilling love relationship.

The distinction between the two states leads us to a journey down a bifurcated path, one road leading to fantasy and feelings, and the other to reality and interpersonal behavior. Because of space limitations, this comment will focus primarily on the latter path, but first a brief word on "feeling in love."

Elsewhere, (Kirschner & Kirschner, 1986) we have described "falling in love" as a regression to a child-like state in which the partner is viewed as a parental figure. Analysts have described the myriad projections and projective identifications with which we endow our lovers. In this condition of vulnerability, rampant distortions about the other person can abound. As Helpern reminds us, we need look no further than the John Hinckley situation to see the possible destructive results of "falling" and "being" in love.

On the other hand, what have we learned about the characteristics

Diana Adile Kirschner, PhD, and Sam Kirschner, PhD, are affiliated with the Institute for Comprehensive Family Therapy, Spring House, PA.

of fulfilling love relationships? In sum then, these qualities tend to flow from an adult-adult relationship, which in some ways is the antithesis of the child-parent experience of being in love. For example, in their study of vital couples, Ammons and Stinnett (1980), found that the spouses showed a balance between mutuality and individuation. Similar results were obtained by Lewis, Beavers, Gossett and Phillips (1976), in their work which compared "healthy," "normal," and "dysfunctional" families. Beavers (1982, 1988) observed that healthy couples share relatively equal power, have complementary roles, and encourage each other's expressions of autonomy. This latter quality, in particular, appeared to enable the couples' ability to negotiate and resolve conflicts successfully.

Another important perspective which sheds light on the nature of optimal relationships is a developmental life-span approach. A good example of research in this area is that of Lyman Wynne (1984) who identified four major patterns of interaction which evolve over the life of the couple. These are: attachment/caregiving, communication, joint problem-solving, and mutuality. We share Wynne's view that the feeling of being in love of which Halpern has written, goes through enduring cycles of renewal and revitalization and is not a static quality of even the most successful couples. Spouses do disagree, have conflicts, and even express anger, disappointment, and a desire to *not* be with each other at various times in their marriages. What we have found, not only clinically but in our own relationship (20 years) is that spouses who are committed to their own personal growth *and* that of the other are more likely to face these difficulties more openly, take responsibility for their own behaviors, and thereby to actualize the potential for falling in love with each other all over again.

Healthy relationships, then, contain *both* the regressive qualities of falling in love and the more progressive adult behaviors of mutuality, caretaking and individuation. In our view, spouses express both the inner child and the adult sides of themselves in recurring cycles. Elation and closeness are followed by perturbation and distance in the dyad which in turn is followed by reengagement and falling in love again. This pattern evolves over the couple's life span. In our book, *Comprehensive Family Therapy*, (Kirschner &

Kirschner, 1986), we have outlined this cycle of relating in greater depth.

REFERENCES

Ammons, P. & Stinnett, N. (1980). The vital marriage: A closer look. *Family Relations*, *29*, 37-42.

Beavers, R. (1988). Attributes of the healthy couple. *Family Therapy Today*, *3*, 1-4.

Beavers, R. (1982). Healthy, midrange and severely dysfunctional families. In F. Walsh (Ed.), *Normal Family Processes* (pp. 45-66). New York: Guilford Press.

Kirschner, D.A., & Kirschner, S. (1986). *Comprehensive family therapy: An integration of systemic and psychodynamic treatment models*. New York: Brunner/Mazel.

Lewis, J., Beavers, R., Gosset, J., & Phillips, V. (1976). *No single thread: Psychological health in family systems*. New York: Brunner/Mazel.

Wynne, L.C. (1984). The epigenesis of relational systems: A model for understanding family development. *Family Process*, *23*, 297-318.

Perspectives on Long-Term Relationships

Roslyn Schwartz
Leonard J. Schwartz

SUMMARY. Loving relationships are developed with the expectation that they will continue. The threat of losing the love of one's mate is so great as to cause feelings of dread. The manner in which a couple characteristically cope with this fear will determine the longevity and quality of their relationship. The behavioral options at the prospect of such a loss are fourfold; viz., changing one's partner, changing oneself, living with the fear or divorcing. Long term, loving relationships can be sustained if each substitutes the illusion of who their partner is for the reality of the personhood of that mate.

"Being in love is like magic. You feel great, you like yourself, you are happy in the present and euphoric about the future. Everywhere you look colors are brighter, sounds are sharper, tastes are keener, smells are more fragrant, and touches are exquisite. People seem happier; they certainly respond to you with greater joy and elan. Even though you are sometimes distracted in your work thinking of your loved one, when you do apply yourself, you are totally involved and generally more efficient. You are more innovative, more "open" and expressive, and frequently more creative. You are in better health than usual and feel firmer, smoother, and sprier. You love yourself feeling this way.

Roslyn Schwartz, PhD, and Leonard J. Schwartz, PhD, continue to reinvent the coupling process, integrating grandchildren, semi-retirement and treating couples in all day sessions into their dyad. Authors of "Becoming a Couple," the Schwartzs try to balance intimacy with the growth of their respective individualities. Utilizing a variety of creative exercises, they help couples, as well as themselves, discover new connections in their relationship.

When you are with your beloved, life is complete. You have everything you want for the moment. You see the beauty in your loved one and have no doubt that it will be there forever. The one you love smells sweet, has a glow that lights up the room. You feel secure, trusting, "at home" with this person. You are more self-revealing in this relationship than in any other. You want to open up and present yourself totally to your lover. You can't get too close. You want to fuse, become one. You can't be together enough. Even when you have unimaginably pleasurable sex, it is not enough. You want to be inside your lover. You want your lover to be inside you. All stoppers are gone. You flow toward one you cherish and, in turn, feel the easy current of your dear one in and around you. There is no question that you belong to each other, for you two are special: you are truly in love."[1]

With such an auspicious beginning why do half the marriages end in divorce? What happens to the energy of this intense connection? One would think that no sacrifice would be too great to maintain such a state of bliss. Yet, in reality, permanent loving relationships are rare indeed.

Interestingly, in over 40 years of marriage and treating couples, the authors have found that both broken relationships and permanent couplings have a similar underlying dynamic. It is called fear. Since all loving dyads begin with both individuals attributing their happiness to their mate, the thought of losing that person is laden with intense fear-actually dread. But it is not the fear itself that generally causes a break in relationships. Separations most often follow from the reactions and counter reactions that occur in response to the fear of loss of the loving relationship.

For most couples the options that are available to them in response to the fear of losing a loved one is fourfold; viz., changing one's partner, changing oneself, living with the fear or divorcing. In most instances the realization that a partner no longer fits the image of the loving mate takes all four forms at one time or another. How one's partner responds to the fearful mate's reaction becomes an integral part of the couple's interpersonal style of relating. The early history of reactions by each member of the dyad to separations usually determines the manner in which they will handle this threat as adults. Because of the diverse backgrounds and reactions to the fear of separation, the resulting interplay between the couple is generally very intense and complex. How this threat to the marriage is processed determines both the resolution of the danger as well as the degree of fulfillment within the relationship.

Some case histories illustrate the reactions to a loss of the loving relationship.

> Lil and Sam are married over 40 years. Except for their initial courtship and early years together they rarely had a good word for one another. Lil constantly berated Sam for his lack of education and boorish manners. Sam felt unloved and unappreciated, and spent as much time as possible away from home. Lil's attempts to recreate her picture of a loving relationship chiefly centered around trying to change her husband. This she did by constantly criticizing him. Instead of achieving her goal she found her husband avoiding her whenever possible. She felt too insecure and frightened to leave the marriage, claiming that she couldn't support herself. While living with her fear and desperation that her life was one endless disappointment, she developed various illnesses and numerous depressions that kept her from seeking greater self fulfillment.
>
> Sam felt inferior and easily intimidated by his wife. He gave up confronting her early in their marriage. Because of religious convictions and a sense that he had not done enough to please his wife, he never seriously considered leaving. Instead, he remained fearful that she would "kick him out of the house" throughout their marriage. He gained some comfort in spending time with friends and members of his nuclear family, but always believed he was on the verge of being thrown out.

While their motivations and dynamics may differ from the countless couples who remain in a loveless marriage out of fear, they do represent those who feel stuck in their bonding and inadequate to find a better solution. Some of the expressed fears of leaving such a relationship are; an inability to afford living alone, feelings that no one else will want to marry them, remaining married "because of the children" and a sense of failure if divorced. What is common in all these cases is that, despite their misery, their fear is too great to seek a more fulfilling relationship.

> Carol and Henry were married 20 years. Their marriage has weathered many crises, most of them triggered by Carol's learning that Henry was involved with another woman. Through the years there had been many "other women." Despite Carol's feelings of betrayal with each revelation she would end up feeling reassured by Henry of his love for her. It always seemed to her that if they could relate better he would not need other women. After the most recent crisis they made a commitment to couple's therapy. Each of them had been in individual therapy and had an awareness of their own needs and dynamics. In couples therapy they confronted each other in an ongoing way for the first time.
>
> Within weeks Carol and Henry were at an impasse. He wanted to be free to pursue his impulses when he was not with her, and she needed to feel secure that he was not "messing around" with other women. She felt she couldn't trust him and he felt he would be too constricted if he gave her the reassurance she needed. After many intense fights about him coming home late and her feeling anxious about the possibility of his being with someone else the therapist suggested that they both date other people, while pursuing their couple sessions. Henry was willing but Carol was initially antagonistic to the suggestion. When they had their next explosive fight however, Carol decided "we'll do it." Several weeks later she had a date. The following day she told Henry she wanted a divorce, and she never wavered from that decision.

For twenty years Carol loved Henry. She loved him even though she was hurt many times over. She loved him even though she felt betrayed. Her sense of security that she had a partner who was as committed to her as she was to him was shattered upon learning of his affairs. This gave rise to her fear that she would lose what she believed was a happy marriage. Carol could only consider Henry's changing his behavior to match hers as the solution to her insecurity. When Henry persisted in expressing his need to behave as he wished when away from Carol, she resisted strongly. She further resisted the suggestion that they both date other people. In fact, Carol considered such a suggestion a major assault on her marriage. She was particularly devastated that Henry agreed for each of them to date others. This meant to Carol that Henry was willing to share her with other men. That was the last straw. She perfunctorily dated another man and then promptly insisted on a divorce. If Carol considered changing her own values to accommodate Henry's life style, it would have meant the renunciation of her basic sense of self. Rather than lose that, she gave up her cherished marriage. Of the four options open to Carol, viz., living with the fear of losing her marriage, changing her husband to comply with her viewpoint, changing herself to agree with Henry's values or divorcing, she opted for divorce.

> Joan and Phil have been married 12 years. After 5 years of marriage, they separated once for a year. Although both dated others during this period, neither formed a meaningful connection with anyone else. They saw each other regularly while separated (they had a 3 year old daughter) and both wanted to reconnect and work at their marriage. They started couples therapy before actually moving back together in order to negotiate some of the issues that had separated them. When feeling threatened by a difference between them Phil tended to pull in and try to control Joan. When Joan started to feel controlled she withdrew and moved even further away. It was because of the anxiety generated by the repetitions of these events that they separated when they did.
>
> During the couple therapy sessions, Phil was encouraged to express his fear and anxiety when faced with his wife's standards that differed from his. Meanwhile, Joan tried to hang in when controlled by Phil and express her hurt instead of withdrawing. The couple was highly motivated to reconnect and both expressed the fear that if therapy failed another separation would be emotionally devastating. They are still married six years later. While Phil continues his tendency to be controlling when anxious and Joan still tends to withdraw, at bedtime they hold each other and then express their respective feelings.

> They promised each other they would not go to sleep feeling angry and distant. They report that both seem able to tolerate a higher level of anxiety about separation, while both actually feel more secure that their marriage will endure.

A combination of a strong attachment to one another and the ability for each to tolerate the fear of a break up in their marriage laid the ground work for Joan and Phil to overcome their respective hurts and share their feelings. This greater vulnerability and exposure to potential rejection was seen by each member of the dyad as an expression of trust and love in the other. Such expressiveness also signified a greater sense of self confidence and personal worth on the part of each. Joan and Phil reported being impressed and pleased with their forthrightness and found it relatively easy to agree to the suggested bed time ritual of closeness In this fashion they both exercised the options of living with their fears while changing themselves. This made it easier for each to try to accommodate to the other without losing their own authenticity. They renounced trying to change their mate as well as the option of divorce. Joan and Phil now have a process to deal with differences between them. Their success in following this pattern has led to resolving several serious disagreements as they continue to grow within their marriage.

Relationships can be long lasting but deadened by the fear of separation and a focus on changing one's partner. There is no real confrontation between the couple because the Pain of being together is less then the anticipated pain of separation. Such pairs can find enough fulfillment outside of the relationship to sustain a perfunctory connection. Through friends, work or a long lasting affair, some couples will stay together with little, or no, fulfillment.

In order for loving relationships to be long lasting while remaining vital, the difference between the respective illusions of who your partner is and the reality of the personhood of that mate must be resolved. In order to accomplish this you have to give up the belief that your partner can make you happy. While the loss of this fantasy and illusion is often accompanied by sadness and depression, it can also lead to a more gratifying marriage. The loss is felt by both partners, even if only one is going through the process. If the wife gives up her illusion, the husband is powerless to reinstate it or ease the accompanying depression. If he is emotionally attached to her, he will feel and share her loss and sadness. Such an interaction can be bittersweet, poignant, tender and close.

What is given up is (1) the idea that you can live happily ever after; (2) the hope of changing your partner; (3) the sense of omnipotence that you can create and sustain a relationship of your choosing; and (4) the attempt to live in the past, with its righteous recriminations, or in the future, with it's expectations.

What you are left with is the knowledge that you have found the strength and courage to trust yourself and your mate to be more authentically spontaneous; that you have someone with whom you can share your innermost feelings without shame or fear of rebuff; that you have a friend whom you can count on to be sensitive and perceptive of you as well as you to him or her. But mostly, you have struggled to create an environment, a marriage, that enables you to discover and rediscover yourself and another.

NOTE

1. Schwartz, R. & Schwartz, L. (1986). Becoming A Couple. Latham, MD: University Press of America.

A Woven Trust: A Commentary on "Perspectives on Long-Term Relationships" by Roslyn Schwartz, PhD and Leonard J. Schwartz, PhD

David I. Perry

Enabling a rapprochement between the members of a dysfunctional dyad through the framework of the psychotherapeutic process must be seen as a primary task for the couples therapist. Unfortunately, even with the most willing of participants it is often a very difficult one to realize. The propensity for the members of the couple to be drawn back into the delightfully delusional hopes, remembrances and expectations of the courtship and early "marital" period can be overwhelming. Maintaining "sobriety" in the face of this powerfully seductive intoxicant presents a significant challenge to the members of the pair. Yet, as is true in so many areas of psychotherapeutic work, the grasp of illusion must be diminished and reality must be embraced if growth is to occur. While couples therapy can be one of the ways in which a more realistic view of the present relationship can be obtained, it is not always an easy process. Sitting across from another person and sharing your most intimate thoughts and feelings can be an extremely uncomfortable experience for some people. Doing this in the presence of, or with, someone with whom you may be having serious problems can be terrifying.

Early in my career as a psychotherapist, I often recognized incon-

---

Address correspondence to David Perry, DSW, 7 Bond Street, Great Neck, NY 11021.

sistencies in the ways in which people related to myself and then to each other, in the treatment setting, particularly concerning issues requiring intimate self-disclosure. At first I was convinced that I was simply witnessing individual differences that I usually rationalized as idiosyncratic to the person(s) I was working with. Surely, I told myself, there were enough differences with respect to the subjective importance of the material being presented by them to merit different levels of disclosure on their part. Over time I began to see that this kind of behavior was common and not only reflective of the types of material being presented but also related to, and often dependent upon, the treatment milieu itself. I noticed that individuals (who later entered couples therapy) would often discuss issues when alone with me that they would only bring up in the presence of their "spouse" after many sessions, if at all. Recognizing this frequently to be the case, I began to use an approach to treatment by which I would intentionally see one member of a troubled couple for one or two sessions and then the other person for several meetings. After this I would invite the couple into the treatment room and the work with both of them would follow. Doing this has been very useful in helping me to understand the problems the couple may be having long before they are brought up and jointly addressed in the treatment room. I now understand that a fear of the imminent or eventual dissolution of the relationship is often operating and inhibiting the free communication of thoughts and feelings. The potential consequences of telling the truth seem more certain with the partner sitting there. As a result, there is a qualitative difference in the communication.

In their article "Perspectives on Long-Term Relationships" Drs. Roslyn and Leonard J. Schwartz map out many of the more common strategies employed by couples in their attempts to deal with the potential loss of their relationships and the effects this may have on their lives. The authors assert that four common strategies are used as ways of dealing with the fear of the loss. These include changing one's partner, changing oneself, living with the fear of the loss or divorcing. Through the use of case studies we are provided with a view of several couples and the ways with which they work through, and hopefully resolve, what are perceived as, fundamental differences between them. While two of the couples chose to remain together and one surrenders to divorce the underlying mechanism by which the fantasy trap is unlocked and the couple is empowered to move ahead is the same. Clearly a more reality based means of communication is used. A meta-communication is established through which the couple can cut across the shrouds of fantasy that each member of the dyad put in place during, or perhaps, before the courtship period began.

The authors assert that a more functional and satisfying relationship may be realized when it is primarily reality based rather than rooted in the early myths of the relationship. But giving up treasured ideas about a partner, even when they are no longer supported by experience, is distressing by itself. Helping clients deal with their disappointments over losing the cherished illusions can be done within the sanctity of the therapy setting when an atmosphere of trust and security has been achieved. It is also in this special setting that the seeds of a more reality based relationship can be planted. Through the therapeutic process a web of trust can be woven to protect the dyad from their Sword of Damocles that threatens to sever their ties. Once in place the web of trust can empower the necessary meta-communication to proceed. This, in turn, can enable the couple to discuss important issues, hopefully, without fear of the dissolution of the relationship. Options beyond the four common ones described by Roslyn and Leonard J. Schwartz, which may not be as costly to the couple, can be explored and implemented.

The joyous, nurturing folly of the early stages of a loving relationship is often wondrous and "magical," as the authors assert. Yet too often the assumptions of expectations, established, perhaps with little thought, during this stage fail us when the magic fades and the anchor of reality grounds us to the demands of life. Fortunately, what we are left with after we have licked our emotional wounds is opportunity . . . the chance to embrace life and our partners as they are and to be experienced, respected and loved as authentically.

And Then There Were Two

Alexander Jasnow

SUMMARY. In responding to the issue raised, that of the factors underlining permanence in couple relationship, it is emphasized that a cultural frame of reference is of key importance. There is a comparison made between earlier and present cultural settings. These different settings are seen to determine the parameters within which such relationships can develop. Contrasting models for couple relationship are compared, those based on constraint and those based on choice. Attempting to take into account the complexities of human relationship, a paradigm is outlined, a description of the type of couple relationship which would be consistent with the nature and spirit of the modern self.

Life for some is a moveable feast, for others, it takes on the semblance of a perpetual fast. I, for selfish reasons having to do with survival and with the quality of life, would much prefer to be among the feasting rather than the fasting. That being established, I come to my second point. I prefer not to dine alone. For dining purposes, two, appears to me to be just the right number. It successfully avoids the loneliness and the isolation of one, while steering clear of the complications, tensions and fatigue of three. The French have given this matter a great deal of study. They do not appear to have come to any definitive conclusions. I personally have noticed, however, that in Paris the restaurants are filled to overflowing with couples involved in animated conversation, enjoying their food and each other.

It is not by accident that I link the concepts of survival and quality of life in developing these thoughts on the issue of longevity in

Correspondence to the author may be addressed to Alexander Jasnow, PhD, 14-11 Lucena Drive, Fair Lawn, NJ 07410.

couple relationships. Survival is a necessity while positive quality of life is a luxury. We have to have bread. It is nice to have butter or jam. We rarely have such options in a time of famine. Which is why Marie Antoinette committed a faux pas when, having been told that the people in Paris lacked bread, she, in all innocence, asked, "Why don't they eat brioche instead?"

With regard to life options, we, in modern Western culture, enjoy a degree of luxury probably unparalleled in human history. We tend to take for granted a degree of freedom in choice of relationship that was nonexistent for most, even in the relatively recent historic past. We enter into couple relationships with expectations and assumptions that would have seemed fantastic, even bizarre, to our more distant ancestors.

In our cultural past, social roles, social norms and social expectations, determined the parameters of couple relationships. People got married not only because they wanted to but also it was what was expected of them. Often they had no choice in the matter. They stayed married because there was no other alternative. Couples, heterosexual or otherwise, who sought to maintain long term intimate relationships outside the socially sanctioned convention of heterosexual marriage, did so at great risk.

We cannot evaluate the factors influencing the nature, quality and longevity of couple relationships without taking into account the cultural and social climate of the times. We are in a period now where individuals experience considerable scope for freedom of action and thought in many aspects of their lives. Perhaps it would be more accurate to say that we live in a time when people's self ideals and self expectations are such that the concept of individual freedom enters into the couple relationship in a novel and radical way.

Where external guidelines exist, it is relatively easy to outline the elements that constitute what is judged to be a good couple relationship. Such guidelines are usually set by long established social tradition. They may be unspoken and unwritten while still exercising an iron control. Or the guidelines may be overt, spelling out explicitly, the responsibilities assumed by each of the participants in return for services rendered. This, of course, simply describes a contractual agreement, in this case a marriage contract. In many ancient cultures such written marriage contracts were the norm. This concept of couple relationship as involving a contractual agreement is still very much with us. We may seek to deny or, at least, hide from view, its more commercial and legalistic associations, but the basic concept is alive and well. It can surface most strikingly when the veil of romantic illusion is torn in the throes of divorce and contractual obligations are fought over openly in the legal arena.

The beauty, if such a term is applicable to a contractual relationship, lies in its clarity. Where such a social condition exists and where a couple relationship is outlined in contractual terms, then a good relationship, almost by definition, is one where each party to the agreement faithfully carries out his or her obligations.

I grant that this is an unemotional, one might say, even cold-blooded, way to describe a long term, intimate relationship. I am well aware that I have not introduced the term, "love," even once in the discussion thus far. Nor have I had occasion to speak of the two participants in this arrangement, as expecting or anticipating self-realization or self-fulfillment. Nevertheless, I submit that, in broad terms, what has been described, is not a total caricature of the situation. It may, on the contrary, be a fairly realistic appraisal of such pairings when viewed from a long term historic and cultural perspective.

As for the elements of self fulfillment and self realization, certainly they could be experienced even within traditional relationships. I say, "could be," as though relationships based on such premises existed only in the distant past. That is hardly the situation. The past is very much with us in the present. It is not only with us, it is also within us. It constitutes a large part of our social identity. There is that feeling of self fulfillment when our sense of self is integrated with and becomes identified with a fixed social role. This may not be the only motivation impelling us to move into a relationship but it can be a very important one. At times, it can be of central importance. We may yearn for marriage not only because we are in love with the other but because we are in love with the idea of being married. We may experience the need to fulfill the role of husband, wife or parent as a necessary condition for self survival and self esteem within our social system. Within this frame of reference, loving or being loved by the intimate other, becomes an added dividend, an additional luxury on top of the social necessity. In the past it constituted a bonus and not a given. In the present it has become an additional element in our self expectation.

Again, I repeat, what is being described is, admittedly, an archaic point of view. Even as I write I realize that what I am setting down sounds more like a sixteenth or seventeenth century tract on marriage rather than anything that has relevance for the present. But if we do not know the past how can we understand the present? This is particularly so since the past continues to be very much with us. We may repress it or deny it but it remains a complicating factor in our present lives. Isn't this the lesson we have learned from Freud?

We live today in a culture climate which can be characterized as one of a state of flux. We appear to be in a period of transition the direction and outcome of which are far from clear. It is a milieu which has affected every aspect of our lives not excluding areas of intimacy and long term couple relationship. Complicating the situation is that even as new value systems emerge along with new self ideals and new self expectations, older values, older ideals and expectations, though submerged, continue to manifest their continuing impact upon us.

Ours is an era of heightened individualism. There is a marked positive valuation placed on the ideal of the autonomous self, whether the self be male or female. It is the ideal of a self that is highly individuated, self directed and self defined. This is a concept and an ideology that is in sharp contrast to that of a self identity defined and experienced in terms of fixed social roles, roles and functions that are other directed.

This is not the time or place to go any further into the complex social forces and ideological movements that, historically, underlie the present existence of the phenomenon we might call the modern self. We are all aware of them in their broad scope since they have affected and continue to affect our lives on a daily basis. They have, in effect, created us. Being so much with us we take them for granted. Like the air we breathe they slip out of our conscious awareness. It is necessary, however, to keep them consciously in mind as a frame of reference. Doing so, we will have a firmer basis for exploring the nature of couple relationship in our own culture era.

The issue of permanence in relationship takes on a very different meaning when we consider it within a setting where individuals operate under conditions of relatively free choice as compared to situations where they have little, if any, choice. This is a statement that appears to be so obvious and self evident as to constitute a truism. What may be less directly obvious is the extent and manner in which these different sets of social and cultural circumstances determine our judgement as to what constitutes a "good" couple relationship, one making for permanence and "authentic" fidelity. The quotation marks have been introduced, not for purposes of irony but, rather, to indicate the essential subjectivity of such evaluations. These are, to a considerable degree, culture determined. That makes them neither right nor wrong in an absolute sense any more than an evaluation of a work of art can be right or wrong in an absolute sense. But such subjective judgements do have meaning as long as we are clear as to the frame of reference within which they are made.

We come now to the central issue, "Within our modern culture what are the factors in couple relationship that make for permanence?" This issue can be put some other ways. "What keeps a couple together because they want to stay together not because they have to stay together?" Or we can ask, "What makes a couple want to stay together, not out of necessity, but because the couple relationship serves to improve the quality of their individual lives?"

These questions would appear to virtually answer themselves. Furthermore, they are so clear and direct as to imply that there must be answers to them that are equally clear and straightforward. But human behavior, as we know, is frequently multi-determined. There is no reason to assume that couple behavior is any less subject to multiple determinants than other aspects of human functioning. On the contrary, the very complexity of such behavior should lead us to expect the opposite.

In seeking an answer to these questions, one possible way to go about it would be to compare different models, different paradigms, of couple relationships. Thus we might contrast two patently dissimilar types of bonding. In one case we would have couples who cling one to the other because of dependent needs. One or both, of them are seen to lack the courage and the self esteem to move into life independently and on their own. They maintain a relationship which may, indeed, have permanence and longevity but it is seen to be based on fear and self doubt. It is a relationship of necessity and not of choice. In striking contrast we would present a category of couples where each partner is independent and self-directing, quite capable of functioning on his or her own, or his and his and her and her, as the case may be. A long term relationship of this type would be one of choice not of necessity. Its permanence might be seen as constituting authentic fidelity.

Clearcut as these models may be, in their obvious differences, I submit that I have set up a straw man. The reality is infinitely more complicated. And yet, it is my impression that, in terms of the contrasting images I have so quickly sketched in, most of us would prefer to see ourselves as independent and self directing within a relationship rather than needy and dependent. This is about as startling a discovery as to realize that most people today would rather be rich than poor, thin than fat, young than old. Nevertheless it is an awareness that has meaning within modern couple relationships. For many, in the past, such an option did not exist. It exists today as a self ideal and a self expectation, a manifestation of that novel phenomenon, the modern self.

There is a great deal of satisfaction to be found in being able to perceive the world with clarity, and to be able to share our insights in unambiguous, categorical terms. To do so makes us feel both wise and in control. Reality, unfortunately, gets in the way. Reality resists abstractions and compels us to acknowledge the complexity of existence. So it is with relationship.

The fact that an unprecedented degree of choice, of freedom of thought and action, appears to exist for individuals in our society, has not simplified the nature of couple relationship. It has complicated it immensely. Whether that is a good or bad outcome for society and for the individual is an ideological issue, a matter of subjective judgement. This is not to imply that people's social relationships were any less complicated in the past. That would be a ludicrous conclusion to come to in the face of the vast evidence to the contrary. But whatever went on within the inner psychic lives of people in the past, on the surface level, that of overt behavior, the scope of choice, the range of possibilities, was highly limited.

Consider a typical mid-nineteenth century, middle class, American or British, married couple. For one thing that sentence itself contains a tautology. What other kind of long term, intimate, middle class couple pairing was socially acceptable or, for the overwhelming majority, even conceivable, if not one of marriage? Within that marriage relationship, the roles of husband and wife were clearly and sharply delineated. The template was crisply cut. Behind the solid, staid and rigid Victorian facade, tempests of emotions might and often did take place. Custom and the lack of alternative possibilities, however, sharply limited the range of behavior as well as the range of expectation.

The situation has dramatically changed. What used to be a fixed tableau of frozen poses has become, instead, a dance with a most complex choreography.

Earlier, in a hypothetical exercise, two contrasting types of couple relationships were presented. One category was described as consisting of mutually dependent individuals. The second, was a category of paired individuals, mates who were, singly, independent and self directed. In proceeding this way a straw man was set up, a deliberately loaded situation. It is in line with a current predilection in our culture, the high value we place on individualism and independence and the parallel pejorative connotation we place on dependency. I hasten to add, as I surely must, that I am all for individuality and independence, particularly my own. Nevertheless, I recognize that to set up such dichotomies as in the two groups described, is both arbitrary and distorting. These are paradigms which take us further away from the reality of the range of possibilities in modern couple relationship.

There is a third paradigm which I see as being closer to social reality, to the spirit of the times. It is one which is synchronistic with deep levels in human personality. Modernism, in its best sense, has not changed the basics of human personality. It has given humans the necessary psychological space in which potentials immanent within us can develop, achieve realization and fuller overt expression. Within the couple relationship this makes for a complexity of choreography never seen before. It is a development that has brought about increased problems in some areas of relationship but, at the same time, it greatly increases and broadens the scope of couple interaction.

Rather than speaking in abstract terms of couples who relate on the basis of mutual dependency or on the contrasting basis of mutual independence, let us focus on a third alternative. Let us consider a model in which the couples are both dependent and independent. Not one or the other but both. Dependence no longer becomes a dirty word. It describes a valid aspect of the human condition, one which transcends age, gender or sexual proclivity. The long term intimate couple relationship is one of the few in our culture to which adults can turn with a feeling of security, and have their child nurturant needs met. At the same time the need to feel oneself to be independent, self directing, capable of making responsible decisions, that, too, transcends age and sex. The issue is not whether people have these contrasting needs. We all have them. They constitute an integral part of the human condition. The problem is how two people go about coordinating these mutual needs within the matrix of a couple relationship.

I see the modern couple relationship to be tremendously complex. It is not impossible to achieve but neither is it easy. Consider, even briefly, the number of roles each participant is called upon to play—partner, playmate, lover, friend, parent, child. Consider too, that these roles must be coordinated with each other. What works beautifully when one parents the child of the other becomes a catastrophe when child meets child. There are also the problems attendant to situations when one or the other is frozen into the role of parent or child.

What is called for is considerable personality flexibility in each partner. It is a flexibility which is the result of self awareness, self acceptance and self esteem. If we can accept our own dependency needs without loss of self esteem, we can more easily be sensitive to and accepting of the dependency needs of our mate, regardless of gender. Similarly, if we value the personality resources of our mate, seeing them as resources for ourselves as well, we have a stake in building our partner up rather than tearing him or her down. We can move away from internecine power struggle and operate as an effective, well coordinated team. The relationship takes on a high value for the participants in terms of survival and quality of life of both. Necessity and choice are seen to flow together in such a fluid relationship. It is a relationship of equals, pooling their strengths, in an atmosphere of trust, caring and mutual respect. If that constitutes an authentic relationship, I like it.

If what I have thus far described sounds utopian, that is not my impression of the realities of couple relationships in our time. It was Tolstoy who said that all happy families are alike while unhappy families are each unhappy in their own way. That has been my own experience thus far.

Let me be clear as to what I am saying. Not all people operate on the same level of competence, personal resource, self acceptance and self esteem. Many couples continue in the traditional modes of relating described earlier, modes in which they find an adequate degree of security and satisfaction. I have described an alternative mode of couple relating which constitutes a goal well worth striving for. It is also a goal which does not call for superhuman or saintly qualities. It is well within normal human capacity. It is also one that is in the spirit of the times. I see these interactional patterns in operation on a daily basis in many couples who go about enjoying their years together, enjoying each other and themselves, at the moveable feast that is life.

. . . Ever Ever After: A Non Scientific Look at Longterm Relationships

Rae Dezettel Perls
Stephen R. Perls

SUMMARY. In this article the Drs. Perls look at twelve couples who have each been married at least 30 years. Common values among the couples are explored including commitment, mutual respect, philosophical viewpoints, and monogamy. Developmental experiences and socio-cultural changes are presented as a framework for understanding how this particular sample of couples continued in their longterm relationships with satisfaction.

We are among a dying breed, the last of the dinosaurs surviving the crunch, a longterm forever married couple. We both are psychologists who do psychotherapy with couples. And we have a friendship circle of similarly long time married heterosexual couples. We asked ourselves one summer afternoon on vacation, "What is there about us that keeps us going along with the same partner?" We started out together in this puzzling process over thirty years ago. Interestingly, a significant number of our current friends are couples who also are married to their original partners for over thirty years. So, we got to talking and thinking that perhaps

---

Rae Perls is a PhD Psychologist in private practice, and is a Fellow of American Group Psychotherapy Association and Clinical Professor in the Department of Psychiatry, University of New Mexico School of Medicine.

Stephen Perls has a DEd and is a Psychologist and Associate Professor in the Department of Psychiatry, University of New Mexico School of Medicine. Dr. Stephen Perls is a Fellow of American Group Psychotherapy Association.

The Doctors Perls live in Albuquerque, NM.

some other folks might be interested in our thoughts about this matter.

Keep in mind that we represent a combined experience with couples in therapy of forty years. We've seen medical students, graduate students, middle America working folks, artists, teachers, lawyers, engineers, other shrinks, conventional yuppie sorts, traditional business types, scientists, senior citizens, gays, almost-married, newly married, never married, longterm married, "open marriage" couples and frequently remarried adults of all ages. One of us sees couples who have been through hospital stays and drug problems, while the other one of us sees a lot of couples who have been married several times, including complex step parenting situations thrown in for added excitement. We have professionally meddled in a lot of marriages!

We have also been privy to a dozen longterm marriages of good friends. These interesting people have traveled, visited, dinnered and talked with us for years about our collective lives. While we never presume to really know what another couple's private life is really about, we suspect we have some significant clues about the differences between our friends and our clients.

Let's first take a look at who these married friends are. This dozen. They are all married to each other for the first and only time. Every marriage is at least thirty-plus years old, and every couple has had at least two offspring. There are no childless couples in this sample. They all started out middle class. Most of the couples thrived enough economically to surpass the incomes of their parents. They are viewed by outsiders as "successful and respected" people in their communities. They all live in urban locations, and for the most part, grew up in urban settings.

All but one couple met while one or both of the pair were in school. Thus, early on, they both knew each other's friends and families of origin. They spent extended time with one another during significant learning and growing years. In many ways they, and their respective families, influenced the personality development of each. It seems a reasonable hunch that there was less rigidity of attitude and style among these young adult couples when they first became paired than is true of many of the couples who marry today. There must be a difference in degree of influence after careers are established and often after several "significant" previous pairings. The longterm couples would acknowledge that their spouses influenced personality development in both obvious and subtle ways. They report having learned a lot of life skills together. From budgeting to cooking; bridge to tennis; theories of economics to foreign languages; these are individuals who grew and altered themselves within the framework of a coupled existence.

Other demographic data is interesting to note. None of the twenty-four people in this informal sample had divorced parents. Many of these friends have thought in depth about the nature of their own parents' marriages. Several of us find those parental relationships lacking in qualities that feel important in this more "self" concerned and "self" expressive era. We know that most of our parents never considered divorce a choice in their lives. Our generation grew up with divorce being more socially accepted than did our parents. Yet, these particular couples never consciously thought from the start that theirs would be anything other than forever marriages, like those of their own parents, but better.

Ours is a generation that experienced gender roles in transition. The explorations and opportunities that these changes stimulated had the effect of opening choices about relationships. Divorce could be viewed as an option where marital discord presents itself. Divorce, for these couples, became yet another challenging issue to contemplate, test against, and discuss. We would "settle" for less than perfect, while many of our parents expected little from their marital relationships, and so settled for less. Many of today's new couples won't settle for anything less than what each one wants. A lot of young people today have survived the break up of several parental relationships, and so it appears, don't assume any kind of permanence. In contrast to couples who get together today, our original dozen assumed they would expend much effort in order to spend their lives together.

Regarding philosophies of religion and politics, this group is rather a mixed bag. While there are several couples with different religious backgrounds, the pairs are in agreement about their current views. Each couple has arrived at an affiliation or non-affiliation with church or temple that satisfies the needs of the unit. Interestingly, there are several Unitarian couples of differing backgrounds. Religion has not been an issue of conflict, rather a matter for exploration and joint decision making for these couples. Even the couples of similar religious orientation have engaged in ongoing discussions about their faith or lack thereof.

Politics has proven more controversial for these longtime couples than religion, although still to a very minor degree. These couples tend to hold similar political views and usually vote for the same candidates in major elections. Only two of the twelve couples have lively discussions about their differing political philosophies. In both the cases, the women are more inclined to be pro-ERA, pro-choice, and Democrats, while the men are more apt to support the Republican platforms. In public, they keep their disagreements very moderated and low-key. In private, they debate more actively. With close friends, there are jibes and teasing about the other's misguided view. They clearly demonstrate their mutual respect and acceptance of difference.

What is most obvious about these longterm couples is that they are committed to the buddy system. They demonstrate the loyalty to connection that accompanies early bonding in pair relationships. Lest we confuse this with the currently popular concept of "co-dependency," we must emphasize the importance of aware choice. Most of the time, these couples prefer the company of the "other" to anyone else in their life. Each of these couples engage in a richly varied assortment of activities with their spouses. Not because they *have*, to, or *need* to, rather because *they want to*.

They travel for adventure and learning together.

They play at something regularly—tennis, bridge, hiking.

They attend theater and musical performances.

Some are active in community organizations, including church.

They all entertain friends in their homes for fun.

They vacation together. Sometimes their grown children join them for vacation time.

Both spend quality time with their children, as they did when the kids were little. All dozen are highly family oriented even though they may need to travel large distances to spend time with their offspring and their elderly parents.

Every person in this sample has served on boards and done committee work either in the community or in professional organizations. This kind of activity is done individually, with the support of the spouse.

They read and talk about the books they read with their partner.

They eat dinners together regularly.

There are times when each person travels without the other, either for business, or visits old friends and family. They talk on the phone when away from each other.

They say they believe in monogamy. Their discussions with others support the sexually monogamous position. If any of them have had sexual liaisons outside the marriage, they were very discrete, for an affair has never been discussed among the friends. If they had other sexual involvements, the couple has kept it very private. Possibly such a relationship outside the marriage has never been revealed. That is not very likely since openness between the pair is highly valued among all these couples. Yet, it may be that the very private agreement to never "go public" in any way about sexual indiscretions, strengthens the bond.

They believe in trusting one another. They are clear that their connection is the primary relational connection. Secrets could be very threatening to the fabric of their relationships. It quite likely that some painful events between them have not been shared outside their relationship. It also seems most likely that these pairs have remained monogamous. Monogamy is most consistent with the way they live their lives. However, we, as outsiders, can never really know about these most private matters.

These are all couples who make efforts to minimize conflict. They tend not to openly fight or argue. Particularly not in public. While these long-married couples are unafraid to openly express differing feelings or viewpoints, the style they have similarly developed over the many years is clearly non-combative. Our couple friends simply do not regard each other with hostility. What do our clients fight about? Sex. Money. Non-communication. Child rearing. Power struggles dominate where there is conflict. These dozen couples are less likely than our client to get caught up in struggles for power. Why is this so? Because there exists in all of these marriages an impressive balance between the man and women. They regard each other with mutual respect and assumed equality. Differences tend to be treated with a good will that grows out of knowledge and trust.

Interestingly, all of the wives stayed at home for some period of time when there were pre-school children. All but two of the mothers broadened their career training once the children were in school. These wives went back to school, back to work, or started in new fields at a time when gender issues were just beginning to be a matter of public discussion. They ventured out of the kitchen before it was popular to do so. We are talking about couples where both partners are strong people. Where strength of personality is mutual and balanced, there is less conflict, not more. We think it is a myth that two strong people will have more trouble in a relationship. Where one person is top dog, there will be a resentful underdog who will look for opportunities to control.

Each of these twenty-four adults have areas of their lives where they are acknowledged leaders. Outside the partnerships, each has their own work and/or volunteer life of some distinction. While observed with the partner, some of these people are more quiet than when they are out in their other roles. Certain of these individuals appear more aggressive in their work roles than as spouses. They seem to have the flexibility to shift from pro-active to re-active, depending upon the situation. They would all be characterized as busy, active, strong individuals. These are assorted spouses who do not provide all the excitement or entertainment for the other. These couples are made up of clear individuals who hold their own, and who share a wide array of mutual interests.

Where is the "down" side? Nothing in life is perfect. Correct. We know these couples have not always been "in sync" regarding career and education needs. Because these were women raised with "old" family values, the male work goals came first and the children's needs followed. Females were trained to have their needs come after husband and children. Where this operated for these couples, as it most often did, there was some "pay back" due from most of the husbands at some point. The couples appear to have survived these particular cultural stresses.

Most of these couples would also acknowledge some times of boredom and restlessness with each other. There have been difficult times for several of the pairs surrounding problems with their children, mostly adolescent acting out of one sort or another. A few of the grown children have had significant emotional problems, probably in about the same ratio as the general population. It is too soon to judge the quality of the partnerships of the adult children of longterm marriages. As educators who believe in the significance of modeling, we assume these kids will have a better than average chance at successful relationships.

As these couples are now well into middle age, they are dealing with life cycle issues. They continue to carry high levels of responsibility both with their work and their families. Aging and ill parents, join with new grandchildren to add demands on time and energy. The couples themselves are looking at changes in physical stamina and life style as retirement is on the horizon. Death and loss issues must be faced.

The first spouse of these dozen good friends died two years ago. It was a painful and difficult time for all their longtime friends. It was a tragic and crushing experience for the wife. It is our observation that the death of a spouse in an intimate, growing, successful marriage is more disruptive and cruel than it is for a spouse in a less dynamic relationship. There is so much more to miss!

It is interesting to note how many of the individuals in these pairings say that they assume they will die before the other. This seems to be a statement of both denial of realities and the confirmation of the strong preference to live within the relationship. Few partners acknowledge the wish to live alone, but in strongly bonded longterm relationships it appears that there is a powerful wish not to be alive without the other.

Maybe the "new" couples expect less of marriage. Films and books have overexposed every possible hurt, and magnified every pimple on the face of marriage. Perhaps they cut their losses and invest less of themselves, because they know going into the agreement that the statistics indicate a fifty percent chance the marriage won't last. A self-fulfilling prophecy of failure? An earlier generation of newly married folks would mostly not have given thought about possible divorce in the future. Expectation of success is a strong motivator.

We all grew up with clear messages from our communities and/or families that successful people "made" their marriages work. Loyalty and commitment don't get talked about much anymore in the popular press. Maybe "hanging in there" just doesn't sound like enough fun. It's clear that a lot of creative effort must be expended to keep a longterm relationship alive and interesting. It may be that couples today would rather switch partners and pay the frontend costs, than look at the long range return on investment. Immediate gratification is popular.

Fear of being "discovered" may be covered by ". . . it's impossible to really understand me . . ." For an other to know so much about me, suggests both trust in that other and a basic security with self. With the sense of failed relationship comes both a psychic injury and a deepened self protection. There follows an increased scepticism that any relationship can be safe and enduring. Nobody really believes in ". . . happily ever after . . ." anymore. However, with the very real threats of death and poverty linked with multiple partners, and the increasing sense of conventional wisdom that the children of our culture are being shortchanged, there may be a renewed interest in how to do . . . "ever after . . ."

Coupling: Contracts, Attachment and Love

Gail Kadison Golden

SUMMARY. This paper discusses the many factors that make for permanence in relationships. Some are practical and relate to the historical provisions of the marriage contract such as economics, child rearing, and social/familial concerns.

Others have to do with attachments needs, the instinctive drive towards safety which propels us to stay near someone who is discriminated as significant to our well being. Dysfunctional attachment needs are discussed as well as the difference between attachment and mature love.

I have thought very often about what keeps couples together when they in fact appear to be deeply unhappy. One sometimes hears about people married 40 or 50 years and we are then socialized to think that they must "really love each other." As a therapist who actually works with such people however, it is clear that this is not necessarily true in the sense that it is probably meant. The following thoughts reflect my work in a suburban community with couples who tend to be formally married. I believe the concepts are equally applicable to persons, heterosexual or homosexual, who are in long term committed relationships that are not formal marriages.

Because we are fed many romantic notions from the cradle, we like to think about marriage as a meeting of souls, or a platonic rediscovery of a missing half (Plato Symposium 191a). The reality, however, often appears to be much less lofty.

Gail Kadison Golden, EdD, MSW, is a practicing psychotherapist and Clinical Director of the Volunteer Counseling Service of Rockland County, NY. She is author of a number of professional articles and a published poet. Correspondence may be addressed to 18 Zabela Drive, Spring Valley, NY 10977.

The notion of marrying for love is a relatively recent historical idea. Before the 17th century, marriages for all but propertyless poor were arranged by parents for the economic and political benefits of the kin group. The marriage was a contract with considerations of property, political security, and inheritance holding great significance. Romantic love was expected to occur outside of marriage and it was understood that this might lead to adulterous liaisons. By the 18th century, individual affections were considered significant to marriage but unions still generally required the prior consent of parents on both sides. Today an individual chooses a mate with primary expectations for love and happiness and residual expectations for certain economic and social benefits (Stone, 1988).

CONTRACT MARRIAGE

In my view, however, marriage remains, importantly, a social contract. In this society it is still the accepted and most comfortable way to provide for the begetting and rearing of children. Although the divorce rate has resulted in a growing number of children who no longer grow up in two parent families, this poses many financial and child care difficulties that we as a society have yet to resolve. Having witnessed the drastic fallout from the divorce explosion of the last twenty years, many therapists I know today who counsel couples with children say clearly: "If you can stick it out for the sake of the children, then do so."

Marriage also provides financial stability and a suggestion of social normality which are not to be dismissed lightly. We are still a couple society. The shared labor of two people and increasingly the shared income improve the possibility of securing some of the benefits of the American dream. The social norms, which expect adults to pair, still govern many of our social conventions and structures. We still, as a culture, wonder "what is wrong" with a person who has never been married. My experience as a psychotherapist is that many couples remain connected because the marriage contract is being fulfilled in a manner that meets many needs of the partners, even though significant emotional and sexual needs go unmet. People may be good wage earners, good homemakers, good parents or well regarded socially. Many people are reluctant to give up these benefits, or do not feel self sufficient enough to forgo the assistance of the spouse and still maintain a good quality of life. Many, many people supplement "contractual" marriages with affairs that can either be brief or span many years.

In addition to functional reasons that people stay married, there are significant attachment needs that can be satisfied, even in a marriage between two people who seem to cause each other great distress.

ATTACHMENT

John Bowlby (1988) defines attachment as a form of behavior that results in a person attaining or maintaining proximity to some other clearly identified individual who is conceived as better able to cope with the world.

Bowlby conceptualizes this behavior as having its own internal motivation, distinct from feeding and sex and *equally important to survival*. The biological function served by attachment behavior is protection from predators. People are safer in the company of their own kind; in particular, a person might derive a sense of safety from one who is seen as significant or more capable than himself or herself. Humans share this behavior to varying degrees with members of other species.

What this suggests is that a spouse may be perceived as providing shelter, security, or some measure of safety in a world that is often experienced as overwhelming and even dangerous. This is true for both genders of course. Men may count on women for food, a home base, sexual constancy, and connection with a way of feeling and relating which can elude many men who are raised in this culture. Many men acknowledge that in these areas, women augment their survival skills. Taken together these functions can comprise an experience of a secure base which makes it easier to negotiate the larger world. Women rely on men for their (still) greater earning power, their physical strength, aggressiveness, and protection functions. It is a reality that in many places, women are far safer in the company of a man than if they go out alone. Thus, the attachment phenomenon, the perception that we are safer in the company of another has both concrete reality and a felt psychic reality.

There are thus many couples who, while they do not appear to give each other a great deal of pleasure, appear to give each other a secured feeling. They tend to seek treatment when a security function is threatened.

Carla sought therapy when her husband lost his job. Their marriage of 30 years was civilized, but in many respects unrewarding. They were unenthusiastic sex partners, rarely shared feelings with each other and had limited interests in common. He was however a concerned father and a responsible provider. He felt confident that he would find another job and put his energies in that direction. She, however, needed a great deal of help with her own level of anxiety. She had no interest in using this time of crisis to deepen the marriage or improve communication. When her husband found a job, she left treatment. Carla and her husband functioned as attachment figures for each other, and though the marriage was wanting in many respects, neither experienced the other as oppressive or depriving. Over the years Carla has supplemented the marriage with occasional affairs. She did not know if her husband had done the same. One could easily call this relationship limited, impoverished or boring but not necessarily pathological. When are we, then, looking at an attachment relationship which is an unhealthy one and when are we looking at an attachment relationship which includes feelings of love?

UNHEALTHY ATTACHMENT

I believe that we are looking at an unhealthy attachment relationship when the attachment figure also becomes a persecuting or depriving figure. Thus, the person who is perceived to be the one who augments our security in the world is also hurting us deeply or depriving us of vital nurture and concern. We see aspects of this paradox clearly in the attachments to biological parents of abused children who wither in benign foster homes, longing for a reunion with the abusive parent. We also see this played out with dysfunctional couples who appear to wound each other on a daily basis and yet who can not separate. One can view such couples as sadomasochistic but I think such a rubric can obscure the depth of the suffering involved and also trivializes the felt threat to survival which may be associated with separation. The concept that the abusing figure can also be the attachment figure assists us in working with such couples in a most patient and compassionate light. In fact, I have observed in an earlier article (Golden, 1990) that attachment behavior is exacerbated when individuals feel themselves to be in danger, because, by definition, people see attachment figures as capable of protecting them from danger.

> This construct poses a particularly painful dilemma for individuals in significant relationships with persons who abuse them. In such instances the danger emanates from the person who is also the attachment figure. This situation locates the abused person in a painful unconscious loop—the greater the danger, the more the person feels the need to secure the relationship to his or her attachment figure. (p. 101)

The following case illustrates some of these ideas.

Mary and Bob met when she was in junior high school and immediately formed a fast bond. She was the child of a psychotic mother and suffered daily emotional torment. He was the child of very self involved parents who regularly sent him away to live with relatives when they felt overwhelmed. Mary and Bob married when she was 17 and he was 20. In some important respects they both skipped over many of the tasks of adolescence. Neither one achieved a strong sense of self or formed a clear identity. For each, the identity was formed in response to the other and as a part of the marriage. Both saw Bob as the rescuer of Mary. He in turn had found someone who needed him so badly, that he felt he would never be sent away again. Now, some thirty years later, they are both in deep pain, and have been for a long time. Mary suffers the deep emotional damage of her childhood which Bob could not assuage. She berates him daily for being imperfect in some way and withholds sex, food, and often basic kindness on a very regular basis. He expresses anger by withdrawal and cutting her off. He berates her for being such a depriving figure in his life, and feels she is responsible for his acute depression, his high blood pressure, and his ulcers. In some respects, he believes that she is shortening his life. Nonetheless the thought of leaving her produces panic in him and he redoubles his efforts to please her. She experiences marriage to him as a severe disappointment. She says that she would never marry him if she met him today. Yet, she can not even conceive of leaving him. "Where would I go?" she asks.

Attempting to treat this couple without an understanding of the way they meet each other's attachment needs would be a baffling undertaking. Despite the many ways in which they hurt each other, they formed a bond in early adolescence as they were attempting to separate from parents, and before they had solidified individual identities. They feel capable of survival together, though each is deeply unhappy.

LOVE

There is no question but that on some level attachment behavior objectifies the other. For although it discriminates between the attachment figure and all others (the foster mother can not replace the mother) the "choice" of the attachment figure can appear random or historical—the person was "there" at the moment in development when the need was acute.

Thus to say that Mary is Bob's attachment figure is not to say that he particularly values her for certain qualities of personality, heart or mind. Nor does he feel he made a good choice of mate when he was 20, nor does he believe that he would choose her again today. What he does say is because he has been with her since he was 17, his sense of well being on some level is bound up with her physical presence or proximity to him. He also believes that many of his deepest needs are frustrated on a daily basis because he chooses to remain in a relationship with her. Yet the thought of facing life without her still terrifies him. She in turn, correctly perceives that his plaintive pronouncements that he would never leave her have little to do with any specific appreciation of her. She feels objectified in the marriage—feels needed but not valued and not loved.

The experience of love is an experience of the other as a subject like ourselves—with discriminated needs, feelings, thoughts, and with unique value. We value the person for specific attributes, for the emotional gifts we receive from them, for the qualities they see in us. We like who we are and who we have become in our relationship with them. They enable us to feel that we have good gifts to offer them and that we enrich their lives in the same way that we believe they enrich ours. We are grateful to them for enabling us to experience our own goodness and for sharing theirs with us. These feelings can certainly exist alongside an experience of attachment but are clearly not the same.

In an experience of mature love we go beyond issues of survival. We all emerge from childhood with residual guilt for unacceptable feelings, thoughts, and wishes (Klein, 1975). We learn that we are not damaging when those we care for thrive or do not blame us when they falter. We learn that we are not damaged when we can love, work, play and when we can both give and receive good things. When we can have these things in an adult relationship, we are healed, repaired, and restored. While attachment is instinctual and is about survival, mature love is about the drive of the individual towards psychic wholeness through relationship with a specific love object.

WHAT MAKES PERMANENCE

Thus there are many factors that make for permanence – some very practical, some having to do with attachment needs, and others relating to true mutual regard. The most distressing cases to work with as a therapist are those in which the attachment figure is also oppressive, abusive or depriving. We tend, instinctively, to want to assist people who are hurting each other to separate. But separation in itself can be experienced as a persecution by someone who feels that their survival in the world is tied to the proximity of the mate. (I will not discuss here the very specific problems inherent in a battering relationship. When a woman is dealing with a violent partner, she may quite legitimately fear extreme physical retaliation if she tries to leave or assert herself.) Thus, permanence in a relationship does not always seem like a good thing to the observer. Yet I am concerned that labels such as "co-dependent" insinuate illness and blame when we ought to be more respectful of the elaborate though painful ways in which many people seek to survive. In some respects, the world *is* full of predators. It is not easy to confront the world alone. Many people languish in unhappy relationships because they do not believe they have the individual resources to survive "in the jungle."

One can say that psychotherapists have a bias in favor of self actualization. This is in most regards, a good thing. The value placed on individualism is a late historical development, however, and does not obliterate long traditions that value family, kin, and social group above all else. Some patients are ready to "go it alone" and put the needs of the self above all other considerations. Psychologically others are not ready to do this and the goal of psychotherapy may be to very slowly and patiently help them grow to readiness for a journey towards self fulfillment. Others may simply work towards having an increased level of comfort or understanding within a very difficult relationship. Or they may attempt therapy several times at different developmental points before they can move forward. It is not easy to be a person. We need to be respectful of the varied ways in which people attempt this most difficult of tasks.

REFERENCES

Bowlby, J. (1988). *A secure base*. NY: Basic Books.

Golden, G. K. (1990, March). Attachment—not dependence. *Social Work*, 35 (2).

Klein, M. (1975). *Love, guilt and reparation and other works 1921-1949.* NY: Delacorte Press/Seymour Laurence.

Stone, L. (1988). Passionate attachments in the west in historical perspective. In W. Gaylin, MD and Ethel Person, MD (Eds.), *Passionate attachments: Thinking about love*. NY: The Free Press.

Facets of the Dance

Petruska Clarkson

SUMMARY. This paper explores five differentiated facets of relationship involved in coupling and couples therapy. These are the person-to-person aspect, the transferential aspect, the working alliance, the reparative aspect, and the transpersonal aspect. It is suggested that these five facets tend to be present in most permanent couples relationships in varying degrees and at different times. This integrative framework is offered to assist couple and couples therapists in the assessment, treatment, and growth of mature, loving human relationships.

Dictionary definitions of *couple* range from "that which unites two, especially a brace or leash for hounds" to "two partners in a dance" (Onions, 1973, p. 441). The experience of being in a couples relationship can also range between these extremes. On the one hand, a couple can feel leashed to another, with the stinging predictable driveness and lack of autonomous ways of escape of such a situation. On the other extreme of the continuum, they may experience the exhilarating spontaneity and pleasant discoveries of a joyful engagement of two partners in the dance of life. Because of the theme of "permanence" in couples relationships in this volume of the journal, the focus of this paper is about long-term relationships.

However, "permanence" in coupled relationships is not to be equated with being necessarily "good" and should not be consid-

Petruska Clarkson, MA, PhD, is a Chartered Clinical Psychologist, a practicing psychotherapist and psychotherapy supervisor, as well as a Certified Clinical Teaching Member of the I.T.A.A. She is also a Teaching Member and Chairperson of the Gestalt Training Institute of Great Britain and Coordinator for the British Society for Integrative Psychotherapy. Dr. Clarkson directs the Clinical Psychotherapy Training Programme at *Metanoia* Psychotherapy Training Institute, 13 North Common Road, London W5 2QB, England.

ered separate from quality. Sometimes very short relationships which do not become permanent may have enormous growthful and transformative value to both parties. Such relationships may equip them to become better partners for others or even to decide to live in celibacy. Permanent couples relationships may therefore be characterized by or culminate in disaster, transformation, blessed contentment, or boring banality. Perhaps even most long-term relationships have elements of all of these at times throughout their history. Generally though, most human beings *long* for relationship and many tend to prefer *long* ones.

Apart from the necessities of physical survival, nothing outweighs the importance of our relationships with others. Indeed research studies have repeatedly shown that even physical survival and physiological growth, particularly in infants and young children, may be seriously jeopardized in the absence of a close *caring* relationship (Schaeffer, 1965; Provence & Lipton, 1962). Human wellbeing appears to depend on our relationships with others. Our relationships are the bread and butter of all human transactions as well as the pre-occupying passion of the world's greatest psychologists, writers, and philosophers.

An integrative framework for couples work includes psychodynamic, humanistic/existential and cognitive behavioural approaches in the individual blend of each unique psychotherapist (Clarkson, 1990). This paper intends to briefly focus on integrating five aspects of the multifaceted phenomenon of relationship as they apply to couples and couples work. These are the person-to-person aspect, the transferential aspect, the working alliance, the reparative aspect, and the transpersonal aspect. These five facets tend to be present in all important couples relationships in varying degrees and at different times. The longer the relationship, the more likely it is that these facets can be cut clearly and each reflect their own unique light on this most problematically animal and most astonishingly evolutionary aspect of human endeavours—the need to mate.

One of the greatest sources of pleasure, enjoyment, and development in life is the *person-to-person* relationship with another person as one uniqueness meets another in attraction, joy, and love. This here-and-now existential encounter between two people involves the greatest degree of individuality and delight in difference as well as the greatest sharing of boundary, of space, of body. To allow myself to be truly entered by you or allow myself to truly enter into you can be the acme of fulfillment in loving relationship. This facet has Eros in the ascendence. In this process of relatedness both individuals become more than themselves. They create a relationship between them which is greater than the sum of both while each is changed as a result of the enlivening encounter with the other. Loving relationship with a long-time partner is often the source of our deepest physical pleasure, existential meaning, and emotional peace.

At the same time, our closest physical and emotional relationships can also be the source of deepest pain and unimaginable torment. Journalistic reports and personal or clinical experience of violence done by parents, lovers, husbands continue to hit the headlines and disturb one's dreams of humankind's perfectability. Indeed one is statistically more likely to be murdered by a relation than by a stranger. Many of our greatest playwrights and novelists have won their acclaim (in plays from *Othello* to *Who's Afraid of Virginia Woolf*) for dissecting the cruelties and madness attendant upon two people who risk the close engagement of intimacy. There are also others (from *Bent* to *Children of a Lesser God*) which celebrate the transforming capacity of love to lift two "coupled" human beings from degradation and limitation to transcendence or even a moment of hope.

Of course, the first couple experienced by the human being is the one formed with its original caretaker—mother, father, nurse, or warden. This first matrix of connection outside the womb becomes the blueprint for coupling relationships for the rest of the individual's life. Naturally, subsequent experiences, particularly the modeling of parents or caretaking grownups in one's first environment, will influence, shape, and sometimes replace these deeply laid down imprints. However, it is unlikely that the traces of the earliest primeval experiences will become entirely obliterated. Early experiences of rough handling, careless neglect, nervous invasion, loving fascination, or sheer delight in another's existence probably continue, for the rest of our lives, to shape or influence our anticipations of what may happen when we enter into relationship or connectedness with another. Later experiences with other adults, particularly grownups of the other sex, also profoundly influence our future relationships.

These partly unconscious, perhaps even visceral expectations of what is likely to happen when we engage in emotionally and physically close relationships with others, subsequently become patterns of expectations, fears, and hopes transferred onto our potential future partners. When unchecked they act as distortions of our adult relationships, particularly those where we are most vulnerable and most "in love." This psychological phenomenon of transference has been studied in many ways ranging from the classical psychoanalysts (Freud, 1912) to the contributions of the object relations theorists (Fairbairn, 1952) to the script patterns of transactional analysis (Gellert, 1983). Technically, the phenomenon of transferring earlier relational patterns into the here-and-now relationship could be restricted by definition to transference in the therapeutic relationship. However, there could hardly be a couples therapist who would claim not to have noticed how childhood experience has a tendency to be repeated or defended against in subsequent relationships with partners. This is the *transferential aspect* of a couple's relationship.

Early experiences of a cruel father lead to expectations of repetitions of, or determined attempts to avoid, neutralize, or deny cruelty in a husband. The man who grew up with an alcoholic mother who never listened to his feelings, marries a diet-obsessed, valium-addicted woman who is too absorbed in her own distress management to pay attention to his emotional needs. Equally, patterns of childhood abandonment or neglect tend to be feared or apparently repeated in a heartlurchingly predictable manner (despite the most stringent attempts to avoid it).

These transferential patterns are often enacted against our best intentions and in spite of our best judgment. Healthy permanent adult relationships are often influenced or even undermined by these early shapers of our interpersonal expectations and experience. The transferential distortions come from the unresolved past to wreak havoc in the present; they erupt from the unfinished business with our parents into the current tasks of couples life. These past patterns which people bring, usually out of awareness, are probably also the greatest forces for distortions, limitations, breakup, and dissolution. Unfortunately, unless the people involved make substantial script changes these patterns will tend to be compulsively, if unconsciously, repeated.

The appropriate forum for the dissolution of the transference is usually the psychotherapy relationship where the psychotherapist's personal needs are not interlocked with or dependent on the other person's. In our mutually 'loving' relationships the emotional needs and historical conflicts of both people are too tightly interwoven to make it easy to unravel into constituent parts. This would be the equivalent of a surgeon operating on her own child—only to be done in utter emergency. Furthermore, without improved insight and psychological change, a toxic relationship is all too frequently replaced by another which is just as destructive, often in very similar ways. Humans often inadvertently choose partners who continue the same scripts, though we try to find better partners who we think are improvements on the earlier prototypes.

Arguably, even when a couples relationship is apparently positive, it may be based more on past experiences which do not adequately account for the uniqueness of one's present partner. For example, a man who was indulged by his mother may acquire a devoted "mommy" (and he may even call her that) as his wife. She may welcome this kind of relationship because she was an older daughter who only found meaning in her life from serving the youngest adored son in the family, never discovering her own needs to be independent and valued for herself and her own talents. These kinds of couplings may work, they may even be permanent. One doubts if they provide the respective partners with the greatest degree of developmental opportunities, or individual fulfillment, or creative potential.

Yet, in all these matters, one should take great care not to judge from the outside what may be deeply meaningful and true for the two people involved. What may seem incomprehensible to the outsider (couples therapist or not) can only be truly evaluated by the subjective experiences of the individuals. Autonomy, growth, individual fulfillment, multiple orgasms may all be worthwhile goals if the individual chooses them. Any or all of these may also become tyrannies imposed from the outside which in their turn become servants of the oppressive forces in life which paradoxically can strip people of their freedom to choose. For example, a woman may be coerced into leaving an alcoholic husband more from the needs of the current ideological "position" (or fashionable approach to co-dependency) rather than from a true choice made for herself according to the ideals of her highest Self. Enforced liberation is not necessarily more freeing than enforced slavery.

Echoes of our earliest relationships survive in most couples relationships whether for good or for ill. These transferred expectations, hopes, fears, compulsions, permissions from the past, may enhance our presents or provide hopeful blueprints for our future. However, to the extent that they blur or minimize the here-and-now experience with this here-and-now unique individual they may be experienced as limiting, obscuring, or destructive. They form the breeding ground for the complaints of most people asking for couples therapy. Such transferred patterns also constitute the common "weeds" in healthy relationships.

For example, one of the most frequent complaints of long-time couples is that sex between them becomes more "habitual" and less exciting. Sex, then, often becomes a neglected part of the relationship much as the couple consolidates gains in comfort, emotional richness, and shared understanding. As familiarity sets in perhaps the coupled partner becomes more "family" or kin than exciting different "other." As the sharpness and excitement of individual differences become blurred into similarities of experience, agreed opinions, shared tastes, common position, well-known bodies, the partner begins to feel more like a *family* member. With this familiarity (if it does not breed contempt) often comes shades of the incest taboo. This can happen where one or both of the partners begin to lose the edge of interest and excitement in sensual enjoyment, sexual discovery, and mutual physical experimentation. They then become more like brother and sister, instead of man and woman, for example. In order to keep alive the person-to-person aspect of our loving relationships in this sense we need to stay vigilant about the intrusion of "family" or familiar transferential patterns which can deprive our present of genuine emotional or sexual "currency."

The third aspect of the couples relationship refers to this "vigilance"—this willing engagement in the task of remaining conscious, furthering in awareness our individual and mutual development and growth in the knowledge that we are fallible human beings, often struggling with our pasts, our out-dated habitual patterns, our ancient fears and ingrained foibles. It is in essence the *working alliance* as it applies to the couple. It is the yoking together in goodwill the best which our minds and hearts have to offer against the regressive pre-determining pull of our scripts. It is the Adult-to-Adult contract which states, for example, that "even if I feel violent toward you, I will never hit you." It is the commitment to remember the person-to-person love and genuine goodwill even when it feels as if your partner is out to destroy and humiliate you in the same way that a vicious parent did. It is the mutual alliance which helps couples to unscramble such destructive or paranoid patterns and which brings them to therapy.

Love is also this working agreement to honor and protect the rational, aware, consciously chosen best in ourselves and the other even when there is failure, betrayal, confusion, misunderstanding, pettiness, and impulses to repeat the destructive or banal patterns we learned or saw enacted. So few of us have the opportunity to watch and learn from healthy, growing, challenging, and loving parental partnerships dealing effectively and creatively with the problems and demands of life. In most cultures we have been inundated with unrealistic, overromanticized images of coupledom in fairytales, films and on advertising billboards. Powerful, incredibly attractive men fall in love with unbelievably beautiful women and then, for all we know, it looks like they live happily ever after. This contrasts so utterly (for most teenagers, for example) with the often miserable, but certainly less appealing reality of ordinary men and everyday women grappling with the realities of childrearing, the ambiguities of prejudice and the stresses and strains of "making a living" in the latter part of the twentieth century.

The fourth facet of relationship for a couple is its *reparative* quality. Much as it is true that our partners cannot heal the hurts and injuries of our past in the way that psychotherapy can, good relationships are in fact often experienced as nourishing and reparative. It is extremely rare for partners to be able to undo the transferential distortions of each other's pasts. This seems to be province of the therapist-client relationship. In a couple's relationship between two equal human beings, where both have intense and profound needs for and of each other, the transferential patterns are most likely to interlock and become mutually reinforcing. However, the healing power of a good living relationship can be profoundly transformative and bring about a true *metanoia* – a turn-a-round in an individual's life (Clarkson, 1989). For example, Lord Byron turned from an aimless, self-indulgent profligate into a serious and committed man in the service of the European liberation movement when he finally formed an important couples relationship.

The redemptive power of a partner's love may be physical as well as psychological. A woman who survived a rare and deadly form of cancer who had been warned that she may have been left sterile as result of chemotherapy stated, with her new baby in her arms, "I've such a lovely life with my husband, Jamie, that I know I'm no longer at risk. Jamie is all I ever dreamed of in a husband. I'm far too happy to be ill" (Hall, 1986, p. 31).

Often this facet of reparative relationship seems to involve a genuine liking for the partner's "inner child" (Miller, 1986). The attractiveness of these psychological children inside adults influences the partners' connection and their fun in playing together. This inner child is alive in each one of us and constitutes a major part of the charm and enchantment of a partner as one delights in the "little boy" or "little girl" who occasionally shines through the mature adult. Loving partners can provide for each other a delight in each other's existence which may have been too sadly lacking in childhood. Although this is not psychotherapy, it can be deeply therapeutic and healing.

Sometimes it may be difficult to see the child in the other (as when in a sulk or a tantrum) and it may be difficult to reach (as when it has become desensitized from terror or has fled in despair). However, the willingness to remain compassionate toward that child in ourselves and in the other is one of the most precious components of long-term relationships. This is not to infantilize the other, but to honor their living past with its hurts and confusions, its likes and dislikes, its scars and its dreams. It involves the nurturing caring for the other's child, even if it appears only for a moment (in a single moment of embarrassment over a mistake) or over a period (spontaneous regressions of grief or illness).

Finally, the *transpersonal* facet of relationship needs to be accorded its place. This aspect of couples relationships transcends and transforms the personal and temporal dimensions of everyday life.

It can be conceived of in a variety of ways ranging from Tantra Yoga to a sincere, if atheistic, perception of higher consciousness involved in human life. It can also be defined in political terms, as in working toward the preservation of the planet or in terms of the evolution of humanity. Peck is referring to this facet of relationship when he defines love as "The will to extend one's self for the purpose of nurturing one's own or another's spiritual growth" (1978, p. 81).

An appreciation of this relational dimension does not have to involve religion or metaphysics. It is present in shared experiences of childbirth, in fighting discrimination together and fanning each other's hopes in the face of the multitudinous little disappointments of life, by joining in appreciation of the awesome beauties of nature and the exhilarating juxtapositions of great art, the ordinary everyday magic of a familiar smile, or the tracks of time around a lover's eyes. For many people the wellspring of their most profound spiritual awareness can be found in the space between I and Thou (Buber, 1970).

These perspectives can be shared with couples or used as an organizing principle for conceptualizing assessment or treatment. Although a detailed exposition will have to await another opportunity, a few selected examples may be helpful for couples or practitioners to work with this material. Since all these facets are considered important for every developing individual human being and for every healthy growing couple, it is important to consider each from the viewpoint of each partner as well as from a couples perspective. Destructive or impoverishing imbalances can occur between the two individuals in the relationship or for the relationship as whole. These are not to be confused with the normal fluctuating responsive or rhythmic movements in a living relationship. It is appropriate that during Henry's illness, William shared his fears and terrors of death and abandonment with friends. This helped him better to support Henry who was grappling with sustaining his biological life processes as well as reliving an earlier traumatic hospitalization as an infant.

When the caring reparative relationship, however, becomes chronically one-sided and, for example, there is only space for one partner's inner child, there is almost inevitably a deterioration in the quality of the relationship and a stunting of growth for both. Tanny had been abused as a child, but did not want to deal with this more effectively in psychotherapy. Instead her loving husband received her outbursts of rage against "men" for years and patiently endured her humiliations and sexual withholding without complaint until he developed multiple sclerosis. He had felt locked into a transferential distortion when unconsciously he was reexperiencing the guilt which his mother ascribed to him because of the "damage" he had caused her when she gave birth to him. He felt that he did not deserve better from Tanny. The reparative vector of their relationship was pathologically one-way. (There may, of course, not necessarily be a causal connection.) Anecdotal evidence among couples therapists indicates that more husbands start extramarital affairs when their wives are pregnant or nursing than at any other time. This could be related to disturbances in the caring for each others' *inner* children and lack of motivation, information, or skills in how to deal with this more creatively.

When a couple is absorbed in the demanding tasks of childrearing, particularly when there is lack of financial resources and social support, their relationship can often become dominated by their shared working alliance. Despite their best intentions, time to have person-to-person "fun and playtime" may become inexorably overtaken by parent-to-parent tasks, concerns for the children and mortgage worries. When all a couple's energies are devoted to work and caretaking others (as can happen with couples who work together in business or in psychotherapy for example), the time and energy they have available to spare for each other frequently becomes eroded. The same can happen when two people become so absorbed in working for a cause that their personal relationship fades into the background as their shared commitment to making meaning in the world becomes all-encompassing. In the case of Shirley and Paul, they accomplished their goal of providing housing for the displaced community, but both lost their sexual attraction for each other. When the task was done, instead of glowing in the pleasant aftermath of shared satisfaction, mutual recrimination was followed by an acrimonious separation.

In conclusion, I believe the five facets delineated in this paper exist in all healthy long-term couples relationships which continue to grow and a disturbance of their delicate interrelationship can result in limitation or damage. These five aspects have here been called the person-to-person aspect, the transferential aspect, the working alliance, the reparative aspect, and the transpersonal aspect. An understanding of them can help individuals and couples in healing or improving ailing relationships and enhancing flourishing relationships.

Each of these five aspects of couples relationship or any combination of them may go through permutations depending on the importance given to these different aspects by each partner. Their relative interaction, balance, and range may certainly change over time and in response to the vicissitudes of existence. Good relationships may exist which do not encompass all of these facets or any one of them to their fullest potential. However, in one way or another, at one time or another, for both partners, all five must be there for the jewel of human love to reach its full brilliance. This paper is offered in the hope that keeping these aspects in mind may prove useful for couples therapists to think about and to plan treatment as they engage in the facilitation of quality in human pairing.

REFERENCES

Buber, M. (1970). *I and thou*. (W. Kaufmann, Trans.) Edinburgh: T&T Clark. (Original work published 1923).

Clarkson, P. (1989). Metanoia: A process of transformation. *Transactional Analysis Journal, 19*, 224-234.

Clarkson, P. (1990). A multiplicity of psychotherapeutic relationships. *British Journal of Psychotherapy,* 7(2).

Fairbairn, W.R.D. (1952). *Psychoanalytic studies of the personality*. London: Tavistock.

Freud, S. (1963). The dynamics of transference. In J. Strachey (Ed. and Trans.), *The standard edition of the complete psychological works of Sigmund Freud* (Vol. 12, pp. 97-108). London: Hogarth Press (Original work published 1912).

Gellert, S.D. (1983). *Nuts come in pairs: All you wanted to know about couples relationships and were afraid to ask*. Huntington Station, New York: Cite Press.

Hall, U. (1986, November 30). Miracle of the anti-cancer marriage. *News of the World*, London: News International, p. 31.

Miller, A. (1986). *The drama of being a child*. London: Virago Press.

Onions, C.T. (Ed.). (1973). *The shorter Oxford English dictionary*. Oxford: Oxford University Press.
Peck, S. (1978). *The road less traveled*. New York: Simon and Schuster.
Provence, S. & Lipton, R.C. (1962). *Infants in institutions*. New York: International Universities Press.
Schaeffer, H.R. (1965). Changes in developmental quotient under two conditions of maternal separation. *British Journal of Social Clinical Psychology, 4*, pp. 39-46.

Love and Marriage and Other Silly Delusions

Jerome A. Travers

SUMMARY. This article examines the psychodynamic patterns that (1) inevitably result in a dysfunctional relationship and divorce, and (2) those necessary understandings and prerequisites which are essential for a healthy long term relationship. These themes include: how to assure a divorce, romance as the urge to merge, the role of the Trickster, the template of the Imago, understanding Transference, the Key to Happiness, how to get unstuck and some comments on loneliness and sex. It concludes with a new understanding as to "Why get married?"

Count Leo Tolstoy was wrong when he said that "All happy families are the same." A better description could be that all unhappy families and relationships are the same, sharing certain predictable patterns and dynamics. Conversely, all happy families and relationships, like happy persons, are unique in their wellness and aliveness.

What are these predictable patterns which lead people in their anger and despair to seek the advice, services and support of a matrimonial attorney? What leads star crossed lovers to end up toxic with each other? Why really do people get divorced? And are there any antitoxins for this process?

HOW TO ASSURE A DIVORCE

The simplest way is to get married too young! This applies not simply to chronological age but to the degree of one's self differen-

Jerome A. Travers, PhD, is a psychologist and marriage therapist in Summit, NJ and New York City. Correspondence may be addressed to 7 Ridge Rd., Summit, NJ 07901.

tiation, formerly called maturity. Sociological data shows a direct line inverse correlation between age of marriage and percentile chances of getting divorced. If you get married at age 16, your chances of divorce are in the high ninetieth percentile. Interestingly, this figure tapers off after age thirty. Certainly a good way to prevent divorce is to enact a law banning marriage before age thirty. This would produce the desired effect. Unfortunately, this tends not to be a popular suggestion.

The psychological reasons for divorce are both simple and multifactorial. Generally speaking, a certain level of consciousness and awareness emerges around age thirty. Only with consciousness can any real decision be made. The sad reality is that most folks walking down the aisle are unconscious, sleepwalkers going through a socially appropriate ritual as part of their rite of passage of leaving their parent's home. Problems begin when sleepers awaken.

Additionally, one is startled at the numbers of people walking down the bridal path who at some level of awareness are saying to themselves, "If this doesn't work out, I can always get out of it." If divorce is an option before marriage, it inevitably will become a self fulfilling prophecy. The availability of the option produces a toxin which will infiltrate the psychic bloodstream and poison the relationship without either partner being aware of its presence or destructiveness.

This alerts us to the danger of bantering about or threatening divorce, which so often happens when couples are angry and in the midst of fighting. Simply the threat of or opening up the possibility of divorce will create a dynamic shift which will poison the relationship and almost inevitably lead to divorce, without any real understanding by the partners as to why it is happening.

ROMANCE: THE URGE TO MERGE

To understand divorce, let us first consider the crazy reasons people get into romantic relationship and end up married. Sigmund Freud, a model for knowing oneself, reminds us that romantic love is a 'transient psychosis.' He meant that while in the fugue state of love, one is literally 'out of one's mind,' out of contact with reality, clinically crazy. And that's why love is so delicious! For romantic love is a time of total fantasy, a euphoric condition which leaves us in a soporific delusion that the other person can make me feel wonderful and happy. Looking into the face of our beloved, we unconsciously feel the infant's bliss at being held and suckled by an adoring mother. In this psychotic stage, we perceive that our depression will be lifted, our vacuous lives given meaning and our loneliness abated. In effect, we feel rescued from having to find any meaning in our lives. No wonder there is such intensity around romance, for all of our psychic eggs are in one fragile basket. Lovers mean it literally when they say "I can't live without you." If that isn't a signal to flee, I don't know what is. While the fate of those star crossed lovers Romeo and Juliet continues to make young readers swoon, we jaded shrinks can only see a couple of histrionic personalities with narcissistic traits, a suicidal risk; conjoint therapy recommended.

What Dr. Ruth doesn't tell you about romantic love is that it is a *transient* psychosis. Typically we describe the lifting of the psychosis as 'The honeymoon is over.' Remarks surface: "You used to be so warm and loving, now you're a cold bitch," or "I thought you were strong and dependable but now you're acting like a wimp." Our idealization of the other in romance lifts and we discover that most frightening of experiences; "My God, this is just another person with a lot of hangups!" Then all we begin to see is the other person's cellulite, pot belly, nasal hairs and strange hygiene habits. And the fighting begins. Romantic lovers are now locked into their *folie a deux*.

THE TRICKSTER MADE ME DO IT

Carl Jung adds to our understanding of why people get married. Jung, from his depth psychology, introduces the notion of the archetype of the Trickster. He is that Jimminy Cricket-character, the unacknowledged dark side of personality, who sits on our shoulder and one day unexpectedly whispers into our ear, "Propose marriage now" and whammo, we impulsively pop the question and we're suddenly walking down the aisle wondering how we got there. Our motives for getting married stem from the dark side of our psyche, which Mark Twain reminds us "everyone keeps from others and especially from himself."

Jung adds an even more deromanticized understanding of what happens in the attraction process of intimates. He introduces the concept of the *Imago*, that image or template in our unconscious, formed in childhood, which we impose on the experience of everyone we meet. The person who matches the template closest is the one we'll be drawn to and want to share our destiny with.

THE ROLE OF THE IMAGO

The purpose of bonding with an other or sharing an intimate relationship like marriage is to heal the emotional damage which occurred in us as children. We all had an imperfect childhood, with some sort of emotional injury. The damage that we specifically hope to heal is that scarring which occurred in our relationship with our parent of the opposite sex.

Now here's the scary part. The beloved *must contain those negative traits of our parent of the opposite sex*, as incorporated in the Imago, for us to be attracted to that person. Certainly positive elements must be there. But unless the negative elements of the opposite sex parent are there, we might like a wonderful person but will not be romantically attracted to them. Isn't it your experience that you know certain members of the opposite sex who are wonderful in many ways but for whom you feel no chemistry? That's because they don't embody the negative dimensions of our Imago.

Being attracted through our Imago with its negative components reflects our realization that this is our last desperate chance to heal our early wounds. The function of this attraction is our inchoate realization that with this other we have a second chance; a chance to change the negative aspects of our partner into positive ones, thereby healing our early childhood wounds. The ultimate purpose of this course in this and all relationships is to feel whole, to have the feeling of integrity, to complete a gestalt and have a sense of inner completeness.

Stated simply, we become romantically and intimately involved with a person in order to change aspects of them, the purpose of which is to result in tension reduction in ourselves. Don't we all know that our partner needs to change? But who of us will admit that we initially became involved in order to change them?

Most fighting in relationships is around this issue: why don't you change, so that I can feel better? It is usually expressed as "Why don't you lose weight, or stop drinking, or come home earlier, or dress better?" The irony of other fighting is that we desperately want the person to change but that we wouldn't have gotten involved in the first place if we hadn't savored their flaws.

ALL RELATIONSHIPS ARE TRANSFERENTIAL

Let us look at that most powerful dynamic of interpersonal relating, the phenomenon of transference. This is the process of actualization of our unconscious wishes. Specifically, this means that our infantile prototypes of a love object reemerge and are experienced with the strong sensation of immediacy. The baby part of us experiences our initial primary care taker (mother) in intense positive and negative ways. Our love relationship with our mother, our first and enduring love affair, is always imperfect and incomplete, a source of great bliss and demonic rage. Mothering is always imperfect; we never got fed as often or as much as we needed, our diapers were never changed as quickly as we wanted.

Our relationship with our mother is all powerful and all consuming; our bonding with her was never complete, our separation from her never total. Our bodies grew but not one of us has fully completed the developmental tasks which the psychoanalyst Erik Erikson describes as prerequisite steps toward authentic adulthood. In effect, each of us is somewhat stuck in infancy, toddlerhood, childhood, early and late adolescence. And so is our partner. Can two babies really feed one another?

Our emergence towards responsible adulthood is one of rag-tag strugglings, incorporating the developmental tools of learning the tasks of basic trust, autonomy, initiative, industry, identity, intimacy, generativity and integrity. Unfortunately, family trauma, loss of a parent, or some psychosocial wounding can leave us frozen, stunted or arrested at some particular stage in our development. This prevents us from continuing in the task of developing towards adulthood, call it having a self or establishing an ego.

Erikson says that when self identity (who am I?) is not formed, hectic attempts and repeated dismal failures occur as one seeks intimacy with improbable partners. When a sense of identity is missing, friendship and affairs become desperate attempts at delineating the fuzzy outlines of identity by mutual narcissistic mirroring. Erikson says that to fall in love often means to fall into one's mirror image, hurting oneself and damaging the mirror.

THE KEY TO HAPPINESS: AIM LOW

And now dear Reader, before all of this sounds too dreary, let us ask: "What makes for a healthy, long term relationship?"

Healthy relationships are rooted in friendship. Aristotle reminds us that friendship can only exist between equals. We have very few models for healthy marriages between equals, especially if they are serious about their careers, and most especially if children are involved. Paradoxically, people enter into intimate relationships not to be with an equal partner, (although everyone protests that such is the case) but to get looked after and nourished.

A healthy relationship occurs when one abandons the expectation of being nourished and emotionally comforted by the other. This requires giving up the infant's style of relating. A healthy relationship is based on adulthood, autonomy and freedom, where each has learned to emotionally feed oneself.

To emotionally nourish oneself is to give up our primitive narcissistic expectation that you will make me feel good. It means abandoning our deep seated dependence viz. "Is supper ready dear? Did you make the arrangements for the party Saturday? Why don't you spend more time with me?"

GETTING UNSTUCK

Adulthood means leading one's own life and wishing our partner full independence and freedom to grow and develop as a person separate from me and our relationship. This means abandoning the fusion, merging and connectedness which spells the death of a relationship. To be fused together results in becoming confused.

The diagnostic sign that one is merged in a symbiotic relationship is anger. To get angry at your beloved because he came home late, she didn't pick up your shirts, he mopes around, she's putting on pounds, are all signals that you're in a symbiotic relationship. Now symbiosis is a parasitical state, one organism living off the other in a coexistence which is mutually necessary and beneficial. The most appropriate symbiotic relationship is the baby nursing at the mother's breast, in which they become not two persons but as the British psychoanalyst D.W. Winnicott says, "one being, each of whose survival depends on the presence of the other."

None of us has fully recovered from our symbiotic bonding with our mother and marriage is our attempt to recapture that rapture. It is also our hope to get from our intimate relationship what we didn't get enough of as infants. Adulthood means leaving Mommy, defusing, abandoning our dependence on nurturing figures for a mutuality of autonomy. Only then can love exist. For to *need* a person means that we can't want them. Need implies lack of choice and freedom. A junkie needs drugs. To *want* to be with the other implies freedom and choice.

DIVORCE *and divorce*

One way to prevent divorce is to get divorced every day. That is, the legal process of Divorce (Big D) can be avoided by divorce (little d). Just as we prevent polio or measles by taking an antibody shot of the offending bacillus, we thereby mobilize the immune system to ward off the noxious substance. Clients come to an attorney for the Big D because they've never learned the specifics of how to do the little d. Paradoxically, it is by being physically, financially, emotionally and socially capable of getting a divorce daily that one prevents the Big D.

People don't know how to get unstuck, so in their rage and desperation they see the Big D as their only option. The legal split simply gives the illusion of defusing or unmerging. The painful unspoken part is that love never dies.

LONELINESS

Simonne Weil, the French mystic and social critic, said that no one should get married unless they can tolerate enormous loneliness. The loneliness of marriage rests on the discovery that ultimately one lives alone, that one cannot be rescued from our existential dread by another. In a similar vein, the Pulitzer Prize winning author, Ernest Becker, hypothesizes, drawing from the German existentialists that what motivates one to marry is an attempt at warding off mortality. It is in *The Denial of Death* that one attempts to stave off the ultimate reality which is at the heart of human motivation; the realization that each of us dies alone. The task of marriage then is to welcome our loneliness and not to run from our destiny and fate.

AND NOW A WORD ABOUT SEX

There's something to Andy Warhol's comment that "sex is a nostalgia for when you used to want it." Sex is exciting to the extent that it is taboo. This is why affairs and premarital sex inflames ardor and offers great promise for the future. What rarely gets discussed is the high incidence of impotence on men's part the day after the wedding, a great shock to all parties involved. Contrary to the cliche that a legal marriage is just a piece of paper, the wedding ceremony itself triggers a whole set of primitive responses and early childhood dynamics.

One of the realities of marriage is that sex can and does become dull. Marriage itself can work against sexual excitement. Consequently, sexual incompatibility continues to be the number one presenting complaint for divorce. Couples need to work against the inertia of sated common appetites in order to libidinize and add naughtiness to their sexual lives. This helps to offset the inevitable drift towards sexual ennui and boredom.

In some cases of sexual incompatibility, often a sexual dysfunction (frigidity, impotence or a variant thereof) will become the focus of the couples' tension. Almost always 'sexual problems' are a statement of interpersonal problems and conflict; usually it is a statement of unacknowledged rage at the other. You can't make love with someone you're angry with. Where a person has not learned to acknowledge and be direct with one's anger, which simply drives the feelings underground, the anger will passively express itself in troubling and confusing ways, e.g., frigidity. When the unacknowledged anger gets dealt with, and the relationship has some warmth and humor, the genitals will follow suit.

WHY GET MARRIED?

Malcolm Muggeridge, the English social critic, in his autobiography, and after his sixth marriage, says that his only life regret was in not sharing a life history with another person. Late in life he realized that it was in sharing a life history, in journeying together, that marriage makes sense.

When the early settlers trudged alongside their Connestoga wagons heading West, they weren't discussing intimacy, closeness, sharing or the joys of better sex. Unlike today's couples, they used their power not against each other but they had power *together*. They were focused on a task, of building, creating and producing. They shared a common vision by which, through a mutuality of effort, they could accomplish more together than alone.

'Work and Love,' Freud said are the hallmarks of the fully actualized person, the adult. I interpret this to mean that marriage, an enduring long term relationship, is a process, in which each person loves her work and is working at his love. When both are operative and in balance, less strain is put on the relationship. This allows for the playfulness and reciprocating dependence which makes life a little less lonely.

REFERENCES

Becker, E. (1973). *The denial of death*. New York: Macmillan.

Erikson, E. (1978). *Adulthood*. New York: Norton and Co.

Jung, C. (1959). *The archetypes and the collective unconscious*. (Collected works: Vol. 9, Part 1). Princeton: Bolligen Press.

LaPlanche, J. and Pontalis, J.B. (1973). *The language of psychoanalysis*. New York: Norton and Co.

Warhol, A. (1975). *The philosophy of Andy Warhol*. New York: HBJ.

Weil, S. (1977). *The Simone Weil reader*. (G. Panichas, ed.) New York: David McKay Co. Inc.

Love and Marriage: An Inquiry into the Longevity of a Relationship

Murray Scher

SUMMARY. An analysis of the conditions and qualities necessary for maintaining a long term relationship is made based on the author's observations and inquiries. Conclusions are drawn from the analysis.

I have puzzled for a long time over what factors are involved in the maintenance of a marriage. Marriage is a complicated endeavor and in our time has become fraught with difficulty. I have wondered if: its fragility is an artifact of the vulnerabilities attendant on an age of stress and anxiety; the progression of hedonism over the last century is the culprit; long term marriage is no longer viable or necessary? This article is an attempt to organize what I have surmised from my professional experience as a psychotherapist (although not a primary practitioner of marital or family therapy), my observations about marriages of people whom I have known, responses to my questions of people who have long term marriages, and guesses as to what causes my own twenty-six year marriage to continue. My intention is to synthesize all this information and then to make some observations about it.

Murray Scher, PhD, is a licensed clinical and counseling psychologist engaged in the independent practice of psychotherapy. Correspondence may be addressed to 905.5 Tusculum Blvd., Greeneville, TN 37743.

REALISM NOT SENTIMENTALITY

Marriage has become major business in our society or it might be more accurate to say that weddings are such. What could easily be characterized as a "bride's magazine" view of marriage has taken hold in many people. Attempting to match this romanticized view of marriage with the failure of so many nuptial bonds has engendered some cynicism but not enough realism yet. The lack of realism about the obligations and difficulties inherent in two people's dwelling together over an extended period of time is often a product of the frivolous manner with which such living arrangements are regarded.

I hear frequent complaints that the spouse is not romantic enough or that romance has left the marriage. This is not to be confused with sex or with love although at times romance is a synonym for one or the other of these necessary but not sufficient conditions for a marriage. In my observation it is difficult to maintain a romantic aura in a marriage over an extended period of time. At least this is the case in most relationships. Certainly from time to time a bit of romance is not only possible but also appropriate if not essential. However, maintaining the level of romance experienced during courtship is not likely and the demand for it is often disastrous.

There is a great need in marriage for the partners to have a realistic view of the relationship, including its obligations and perils, in order to insure its success. This view should eschew sentimentality, not the sentiment which develops over the extended time they live together and is a product of their history together, but the sentimentality that is mawkish, founded in Victorian illusions of the bloodless sanctity of a marriage. Victorian thinking is naive and foolishly optimistic. It is or at least has been maintained by a "Hollywood" kind of manipulation of our romantic fantasies. This is certainly less the case than it once was but the overwhelming emphasis of the last several national administrations on "family values" has helped to foster many of the illusions under which our culture has dwelled for far too long.

I am not suggesting an end to sentiment but rather a more realistic assessment of the obligations and realities of marriage in an attempt to dampen the disillusionment which often causes marriages to founder. If spouses grasp the limits and liabilities of their marriages they stand a better chance of staying in them and benefiting from what is available rather than being disappointed when their unrealistic expectations are not fulfilled.

APPRECIATING, VALUING AND RESPECTING THE SPOUSE'S FREEDOM

Most people marry because they want someone to call their own. This is a most understandable yearning, the yearning for a deep, intimate, and lasting connection. Unfortunately, the manner in which most individuals act on this desire is through unrealistic demands for or expectations of attention from the spouse. The freedom of movement of the spouse is therefore considerably restricted.

In a relationship where the freedom of the spouse is respected that person will feel able to create a life that is satisfying and fulfilling. He or she will be inclined to include the spouse in that life because it is an option, not a requirement. In the long run most people become quite restive when forced to live with demands that constrict basic independence.

In a relationship where the freedom of the spouse is valued that person will feel an enhanced sense of self plus the security necessary to maintain the primary marital relationship. This situation eventuates from the growth producing qualities of experiencing confirmation of one's ability to control and determine one's own life by someone who is loved and respected. This sense of being valued will likely lead to a reciprocation of valuing which will be salutary for the other spouse.

The combination of having one's freedom appreciated, valued, and respected initially creates a mutuality of positive feeling. It further causes each spouse to realize that she or he is in the marriage because of wish, not requirement, which in turn creates greater respect for and dedication to the relationship. The positive regard for the spouse's freedom causes that person to be a more responsive and willing partner in dealing with the difficulties which confront all married couples. Without such regard couples often feel imprisoned by requirements and demands and lacking in nurturance and support.

ACCEPTANCE OF EMOTIONALLY INTIMATE EXTRAMARITAL RELATIONSHIPS

It is a commonly held myth that each spouse should provide all that the other spouse needs in terms of intimacy, support, and friendship. This is not only virtually impossible but also a dreadful bore. The assumption creates inappropriate expectations and demands as well as feelings of failure and guilt culminating in anger and recriminations. Although a particular person may be an ideal romantic partner he or she is not likely also to be an ideal emotional support or the best person to commiserate about failed business deals or hurt feelings. This is not an indictment of the spouse but rather a reasonable assessment of the strengths or weaknesses possessed. What one is, is simply what one is and that is not cause for condemnation or disappointment necessarily.

Most of us who enter into a marriage have come there after a long road of friendships and intimate emotional relationships. It is necessary to maintain those kinds of interactions with people outside the marriage. They do not weaken the marriage, rather they strengthen it as they alleviate pressure on the partner and help the other spouse to experience more complete support and emotional intimacy than if reliance were simply on one person.

Maintaining intimate relationships outside of marriage is especially important with members of the other sex. A wife cannot be all things to her husband and his emotionally deep relationships with other women will help him to experience a fuller and more evolved sense of self and satisfaction. The same is true for women many of whom come to marriage with male friends. It is essential that these friendships or others like them continue. Marriages are enriched by such connections, not diminished.

The difficulty in maintaining such friendships is usually the jealousy that arises. It is hard for our culture to conceive of a man and a woman having a friendship without there being sexual intimacy. Fortunately, that prejudice is changing, but neither fast enough nor completely enough. Many individuals as a result of their own sense of inadequacy demand that their spouses relinquish all opposite sex relationships and many same sex relationships. They often seem insatiable where the spouse is concerned and thus find it necessary to demand total fealty. This is unfortunate and shortsighted but nonetheless prevalent.

My own experience is that my wife and I have had numerous friendships and this has helped us by taking a good deal of the pressure off each of us. I have relied on my wife's friends to be supportive and loving of her when I could not or would not. I know she has counted on my friends to get me through crises that she was less well equipped to deal with than they. We have returned to each other more complete and feeling better because we felt loved, supported, and understood by more than one person. We do not always like each other's intimates but we try to respect and value those persons and we know that those interactions are to our partner's benefit and thus ultimately to our own.

MOVING FAR AWAY FROM PARENTS

Ours is geographically a very mobile society. Oftentimes couples move away from the place where they grew up. Depending on the educational/professional status of the couple this happens at differing times in their married life. It is my belief that the best time to leave the parental environs is immediately upon getting married. We are all tied to our parents by many strings. These strings are of varying thicknesses and lengths. Newly married couples can sometimes become so entangled in these strings that their breath is severely restricted if not completely cut off. Parents, in most cases, mean no harm but nonetheless make subtle and unsubtle demands on their children and this can cause chaos.

Relocating at a distance sufficiently great to preclude random and frequent visits by parents or to parents is a most helpful arrangement in a marriage. This arrangement allows the couple to rely on themselves and each other for solving problems and dealing with the difficulties of daily life without the destructive support of parents determined to defend their offspring against the interloper. Couples are helped by creating a life together without the dead hand of the past which is personified by parents who usually have difficulty seeing beyond their own experience. They generally have a very biased view and thus are not a good source of assistance even though it is frequently to parents that couples turn. In this age of rapid communication parents will still be available but the distance will reduce their power. Parenthetically, I would suggest that couples agree that they do not have to like each other's parents but they have to be civil and respectful. This will likely reduce a large amount of potential tension and eliminate a goodly number of pointless arguments.

VIEWING DIVORCE AS UNACCEPTABLE

It is most unfortunate that divorce is commonly seen as an acceptable option. It is certainly true that some marriages should be dissolved as people ought not be required to dwell in misery. However, I believe that the social acceptability of divorce and its increasing prevalence in the world have caused a very different reaction to it than was once the case. If one knows that getting out of a marriage is always a viable possibility that has to change the individual's attitudes toward maintaining and strengthening the marriage.

I am not espousing a mindless support of "family values" in the vein of conservative demagoguery. I do not believe that simply endorsing a set of values will change behavior. Behavior is conditioned to some extent by expectations and permissions embedded in our culture. Therefore, as divorce is fairly run-of-the-mill it becomes an element in the contemporary psyche and has few of the negative sanctions and connotations it once did.

If a couple believes that divorce is something resorted to only in the most extreme situations and that their goal is to avoid it at all costs, they will take their marriage more seriously and work harder at preserving it. Of course, when a marriage is in trouble most young people need assistance in changing things, as it is rare for them to have learned effective conflict resolution either through schooling or through observation of their own parents. It is most unfortunate that marriage licenses do not come with an operator's manual.

APPRECIATION FOR SHARED HISTORY

One of the values of a long term relationship is the opportunity to relish mutual experiences. This includes experiences of both a marvelously intimate nature as well as superficial participation in the amusing or poignant. When a longtime association ends there is no longer opportunity to relive shared memories together.

It is important to note that shared history also includes expectations and hopes, plans and goals. An intimate mingling of such dreams can be a powerful bond between people and a suitable appreciation of that can help in preserving and sustaining a relationship.

In marriages that involve people who are relatively young there is the opportunity to grow up together. This also provides a chance to commingle understandings and realizations as well as historical events and experiences. If the spouses can allow each other the freedom to grow and to share their growth there may be a strong bond which will aid in the longevity of the marriage. Where the marriage is between two people not so young there is an opportunity to share acquired wisdom and the wisdom that is acquired from a late marriage. In either case, young or old, an appreciation of shared experience and knowledge gained is potential cement for the marriage.

LACK OF RESPONSIBILITY FOR SPOUSE'S BEHAVIOR

There is an unfounded belief among many couples that they are each responsible for the other's behavior. This causes them to feel guilty, ashamed, angry, and disappointed when the spouse behaves in such a manner as to offend their own sensibilities or beliefs about how people ought to behave. This mistaken belief in responsibility causes much strife. In reality our spouses are other people who are free to behave badly, the only possible reflection on us is that we chose to marry this person through some error of judgment. If each spouse accepts the lack of responsibility there will be no need to feel bad about the self but rather freedom to express displeasure or disapproval for behaviors deemed inappropriate, hurtful, and/or foolish.

Yielding responsibility for the spouse's behavior enables one to see that behavior more clearly and less judgmentally. This reduces the likelihood of discord. Spouses who do not feel obligated to insure the partner's good behavior usually have interactions freer of argument than those who do feel so obligated. They also usually have less of a couple front and are more likely to be autonomous and to venture out on their own. This relieves some pressure on the marriage and makes for healthier interdependence.

GOOD ROLE MODELS AND GOOD FRIENDS

Those couples lucky enough to have good role models or wise enough to choose them are at an advantage. Most of what we learn about marriage is from our parents and that is not always the best source of information and emulation for long term relationships. People who are in the presence of couples who have worked hard at their marriages will have the advantage of seeing how it can be worked out. Those who have not will be deprived of such an opportunity.

It is usually other couples who socialize new couples into the world of partnership. Again those couples blessed with good models in the form of good friends will do better than those surrounded by couples struggling and foundering. If possible it is helpful to have as friends somewhat older couples who can be a source of information, reassurance, and support. This unfortunately may be a matter of luck in terms of who the friends and acquaintances are but it is also possible to be deliberate about choosing people with whom to associate.

PERSONAL QUALITIES THAT AID IN MAINTAINING A MARRIAGE

Marriage is usually a struggle as there are a great number of pressures on each partner as an individual as well as a great number of pressures on the couple. The difficulties inherent in two individuals with different gender scripts attempting to live together also plays a role. A variety of personal qualities can aid the partners in maintaining their marriage. Some of these qualities can be learned or at least can be emphasized by the spouses.

A sense of humor is essential. So many incidents try one's patience in marriage that being able to laugh at oneself and at the inherent tribulations of a long term relationship is essential. A sense of humor here is also bound up with a sense of proportion. In conjunction with this, a sense of the absurd will be a very great help. There is so much absurdity in the demands of each spouse and even more in the demands of family and community that recognizing the absurd will be of inestimable value.

The other quality that seems necessary is that of toughness. Each person in a long term relationship will have to be resolute in commitment to the partnership and strong in maintaining that commitment. A toughness in the face of difficulty, supersensitivity, and insensitivity is necessary to cope with the trials of living together. Toughness in the face of insult is often important; our partners can deeply offend us, usually unwittingly, because we are so vulnerable to them and have exposed ourselves in many ways.

CHILDREN

Offspring can be a very valuable and fulfilling part of life and marriage. They can also be a reef upon which the ship of partnered bliss founders. Often couples are not clear about their feelings and desires in regard to children and therefore cannot or do not attempt to work through their priorities and expectations. This can create many difficulties. The wish to procreate as well as the meaning of children in one's life are very powerful and influence us, often unconsciously, far more significantly than we would ever anticipate.

How couples deal with their children and with each other in terms of the children is a complex and important consideration. The importance and complexity of the issue put it beyond the scope of this article except for two caveats. First, it is essential that couples initiate a dialogue early in their relationship about children and maintain that dialogue during the child rearing years so as to avoid as many pitfalls as possible. This includes couples who have children from former marriages. Second, it is imperative that couples understand that there are significant differences created in a relationship when there is more than one child. Couples with only children have much different interactions than those with two or more children. Families with more than one child are frequently less manageable and there is a greater emphasis on the family than on the couple. With no children or one child the couple tends to remain more involved with each other.

CONCLUSIONS

It is all too obvious that marriage seldom proves to be the blissful wedding of two souls and hearts in a vine covered cottage that our fantasies have been nurtured to expect. Rather it is a struggle between two individuals who usually love each other but strive to realize their personal dreams and expectations of what this relationship is to be. This prompts several observations about marriage.

First, it is difficult. Marriage is a complicated exercise in two people living together in a manner that is individually and mutually satisfying. It is not easily accomplished and is a process; therefore it takes constant attention.

Second, it takes hard work and effort. It is far from easy to understand one's own wishes and desires; even harder to grasp and accept the wishes and desires of another person. In order to stay in touch with the partner's expectations one must devote energy. The modification of one's own predilections is also difficult but frequently essential in order to dwell together successfully. Exploring, compromising, and adjusting are not easy tasks but are essential to a rewarding relationship.

Third, it is very rewarding. Marriage can provide that complementarity of being and rescue from loneliness that most people seek. It can also provide a variety of life experiences that are joyous and meaningful. Marriage is an institution that can round out and complete a good deal of one's life and so is much sought after, and with good reason.

Fourth, it is hard to believe it can work. The legacy of this century is that marriage is not really viable if one looks at statistics and a plethora of media reports. Nonetheless people still seem to marry with regularity and with abandon. Perhaps the fear of being alone or lonely as well as some basic desire to pair off counteract the disbelief in the viability of marriage. If this is the case it is fortunate as marriage is viable with appropriate effort.

Fifth, it is often not what we might hope or expect but it can be marvelous. Our fantasies rarely match reality and in the case of marriage it would be to our benefit if we would allow it to be what it is rather than what we would like it to be. Then we could deal with what we have instead of with trying to realize our fantasies which only results in disappointment and anger. Marriage promises us great gain and satisfaction if only we notice the joy attendant to living with, caring for, and loving another person even though such mutuality exposes that person's shortcomings as well as our own. There is no perfection in this world and the senseless pursuit of it dooms us to disappointment and dismay, a very sad outcome considering the potential for joy and fulfillment.

Realism Not Sentimentality

Lynn Pearlmutter

I agree with many of the opinions set forth in "Love and Marriage: An Inquiry into the Longevity of a Relationship." The author's views seem less an "inquiry" than an attempt to answer the question "What Makes for Permanence?" When Scher advocates for realism as opposed to sentimentality, I recognized a position of my own. When training therapists to work with couples, I often articulate the importance of a disavowal of romantic illusion about relationships. I agree that humor and an appreciation for the shared history of partners are forces which preserve connections. I also agree with Scher's position of limiting the divorce option. Too often therapists support dissolution of relationships.

Scher writes from the masculine voice when he repetitively articulates the value of autonomy in relationships. In two sections—Appreciating, valuing and respecting the spouse's freedom and Acceptance of emotionally intimate extramarital relationships—he espouses separateness more than connectedness and his position reinforces the research done on gender differences (Gilligan, 1982; Bezzoff, 1989; Belenky, Clinchy, Goldberger & Tarule, 1986). Traditionally men have usually placed a greater value on preserving their independence within relationships than women have. I do not disagree with the value of autonomy within relationships. My concern could be phrased in Scher's own terminology: "realism not sentimentality."

The likelihood that partners of either gender could tolerate the degree of autonomy Scher advocates would seem to be dependent upon the levels of "differentiation of self" (Bowen, 1978; Kerr,

Lynn Pearlmutter, DSW, is affiliated with the Tulane University School of Social Work, New Orleans, LA 70118.

1981) achieved by the individuals within the couple. In my opinion, Scher's autonomy stance could be tolerated only by those individuals whose differentiation of self was on the high end of the continuum, a level reached by few. I disagree with Scher's assertion that young couples need to achieve their disentanglements by moving a sufficient geographical distance from families of origin. I worked with a Chinese immigrant couple whose families of origin lived in Taiwan. They were unable to make an independent decision without first writing home. Although the cultural determinants may be particularily strong in this situation, it is perhaps the most graphic example of why I believe geographical distance is a pseudosolution. Familial loyalties and entanglements are not dissolved by geographical distance. Just as therapists too often support dissolution of marriage, many also advocate "cutoff" from family of origin. To achieve the differentiation of self that, in turn, makes permanence in relationships possible, partners need to work simultaneously on the differentiation of self from family of origin and their connection with each other. Only then can a relationship hope to achieve that elusive balance between connection and autonomy.

REFERENCES

Belenky, M.F., Clinchy, B.M., Goldberger, N.R. & Tarule, J.M. (1986). *Women's ways of knowing*. New York: Basic Books.

Berzzoff, J. (1989). From separation to connection: Shifts in understanding women's development. *Affilia, 4* (1), 45-58.

Bowen, M. (1978). *Family therapy in clinical practice*. Northvale, NJ: Jason Aronson.

Gilligan, C. (1982). *In a different voice: Psychological theory and women's development*. Cambridge, MA: Harvard University Press.

Kerr, M. (1981). Family system's therapy. In A. Gurman & D. Kniskern (Eds.), *Handbook of family therapy*. New York: Brunner/Mazel.

For Product Safety Concerns and Information please contact our EU representative GPSR@taylorandfrancis.com
Taylor & Francis Verlag GmbH, Kaufingerstraße 24, 80331 München, Germany

www.ingramcontent.com/pod-product-compliance
Ingram Content Group UK Ltd.
Pitfield, Milton Keynes, MK11 3LW, UK
UKHW022157190926
475702UK00003B/81
* 9 7 8 1 1 3 8 8 1 4 1 8 9 *